Dättner Jacobson, Moses Rintel

Historical Sketch of the Two Melbourne Synagogues

Dättner Jacobson, Moses Rintel

Historical Sketch of the Two Melbourne Synagogues

ISBN/EAN: 9783337112356

Printed in Europe, USA, Canada, Australia, Japan

Cover: Foto ©ninafisch / pixelio.de

More available books at **www.hansebooks.com**

HISTORICAL SKETCH

OF THE

TWO MELBOURNE SYNAGOGUES:

By MAURICE BRODZKY

TOGETHER WITH

SERMONS PREACHED

BY THE

REV. DR. DÄTTNER JACOBSON

AND THE

REV. MOSES RINTEL.

Melbourne:
A. & W. BRUCE, 68 ELIZABETH STREET.
5638—1877.

A. L. HENRIQUES & CO., PRINTERS, NO. 7 POST OFFICE PLACE.

PREFACE.

In presenting to the Jewish public this publication, in which I attempt to give some facts relating to the formation and progress of the two Metropolitan Congregations, I deem it necessary to make a few preliminary remarks to the reader.

The sources from which I have gathered the information relating to the Melbourne Synagogues are, viz.:—"The Voice of Jacob," local newspapers, printed law books, and minute books of the two congregations. These documents, so to speak, form the *Historia scripta* of the Jews of this city. However, fortunately, there also exists a *Historia non scripta*, of which several of the early colonists are the repositaries. Their information has been invaluable to me, inasmuch as it has led me to make the most searching inquiries respecting a matter which is of great importance to those who take an interest in the early history of Judaism in this great Southern city.

Some months ago the Committee of the Melbourne Hebrew Congregation had placed in an anteroom of the Synagogue a memorial stone, on which are inscribed the names of the Past Presidents, and the name of Mr. SOLOMON BENJAMIN appears thereon as having had the honor of holding the position of President at the foundation of the Synagogue. That honor is claimed for the late Mr. A. H. HART. I, however (who, as Horace would say, "*historiam scribo*") have so thoroughly investigated the matter that I am satisfied beyond all doubt as to whom that honor is due; and in order to free myself from any charge of partiality, I publish a *fac simile* of the title-page of the first law book, and extracts from other documents, which will be found to fully corroborate any statement I may have made.

Extract from First Minute Book, lately discovered.

"Minutes of proceedings according the adoption at a General Meeting of the Jewish Congregation, held at Mr. A. H. Hart's residence, on Sunday, the 12th September, 1841 :—

"Proposed by Mr. A. H. Hart, and resolved, that the Society for the relief of the poor and infirm Jews be dissolved from the present date.— Carried.

"Proposed by Mr. A. H. Hart, and seconded by Mr. M. ~~Lyons~~, and finally resolved, that a Society be formed and called the 'Jewish Congregational Society.' The following gentlemen were then elected by a majority of voices to act as officers for the ensuing year :—

      Mr. M. CASHMORE, President

      Mr. S. BENJAMIN, Vice-President.

      Mr. M. LAZARUS,
       ,,   LINCOLN,
       ,,   FONSAKER,   } Committee.
       ,,   H. DAVIS,

      Mr. L. DAVIS, Secretary.

Extract from page 5 of the first Law Book.

"At a General Meeting held on Sunday, the (20th day of 'Tiveth, 5604, a.m.) 21st day of January, 1844, it was unanimously resolved—That this congregation be designated

קהל קודש שארית ישראל

"'The Holy Congregation of a Remnant of Israel.'"

Extract of Minutes.

"Sunday, 21st January, 5604, a.m.—1844.

"At a General Meeting held this day, at the residence of Mr. A. H. Hart, the Laws, as prepared by the Committee, were read *seriatim*, and after some verbal amendments, unanimously approved of."

"Sunday, 28th January, 5604, a.m.—1844.

"At a General Meeting held this day, at the residence of Mr. A. H. Hart, the foregoing Laws, as amended, were read and unanimously confirmed."

[FAC SIMILE.]

LAWS

AND

REGULATIONS

OF THE

קהל קודש שארית ישראל

"HOLY CONGREGATION OF A REMNANT OF ISRAEL."

MELBOURNE:

ESTABLISHED ANNO MUNDI, 5604.

(1844.)

MELBOURNE:
PRINTED BY W. CLARKE, AT THE PORT PHILLIP HERALD OFFICE.
1844.

[FAC SIMILE.]

OFFICERS AND COMMITTEE.

PRESIDENT:

MR. A. H. HART.

TREASURER:

MR. S. BENJAMIN.

COMMITTEE:

MESSRS. JOHN HART,   MESSRS. EDWARD HART,
J. L. LINCOLN,   JOHN LEVY.

HONORARY SECRETARY:

MR. M. CASHMORE.

It will thus be seen that Mr. A. H. Hart was the first President of the קהל קדש שארית ישראל Congregation.

MAURICE BRODZKY.

Melbourne Athenæum, September, 1877—5638.

PRESIDENTS AND TREASURERS

OF THE

Melbourne Hebrew Congregation,

FROM ITS FOUNDATION.

Year.	President.	Treasurer.
1843-4	A. H. HART	S. BENJAMIN
1844-5	A. H. HART	S. BENJAMIN
1845-6	A. H. HART	S. BENJAMIN
1846-7	S. BENJAMIN	M. BENJAMIN
1847-8	A. H. HART	M. BENJAMIN
1848-9	A. H. HART	M. BENJAMIN
1849-50	A. H. HART	E. ELLIS
1850-1	M. CASHMORE	M. BENJAMIN
1851-2	D. BENJAMIN	S. BENJAMIN
1852-3	D. BENJAMIN	‡S. BENJAMIN
		E. HART
1853-4	*D. BENJAMIN	M. CASHMORE.
	E. COHEN	
1854-5	*A. H. HART	I. HART
	M. CASHMORE	

* Resigned 2nd April, 1854.   ‡ Resigned 5th Dec., 1852.
* Resigned 12th Nov., 1854.

Year.	President.	Treasurer.
1855-6	E. COHEN	I. HART
1856-7	E. COHEN	I. HART
1857-8	M. CASHMORE	‡A. E. COHEN
		J. LEVY.
1858-9	*M. CASHMORE	J. LEVY
	E. ELLIS	
1859-60	E. COHEN	I. LYONS
1860-1	E. COHEN	B. BENJAMIN
1861-2	I. LYONS	E. ISAACS
1862-3	E. ISAACS	H. HORWITZ
1863-4	H. HORWITZ	S. LAZARUS
1864-5	H. HORWITZ	S. LAZARUS
1865-6	S. LAZARUS	S. SOLOMON
1866-7	E. COHEN	J. AARONS
1867-8	E. COHEN	B. BENJAMIN
1868-9	B. BENJAMIN	W. HEYMANSON
1869-70	B BENJAMIN	‡W. HEYMANSON
		I. JACOBS
1870-1	B. BENJAMIN	H. P. HARRIS
1871-2	B. BENJAMIN	H. P HARRIS
1872-3	B. BENJAMIN	S. COHEN
1873-4	S. COHEN	M. MARKS
1874-5	S. COHEN	M. MARKS
1875-6	S. COHEN	L. M. MYERS
1876-7	L. M. MYERS	B. BENJAMIN
1877-8	L. M MYERS	B. BENJAMIN

* *Resigned 3rd May, 1859.*

† *Resigned 16th May, 1858.*
‡ *Resigned 24th Oct, 1869.*

THE JEWS IN THEIR DISPERSIONS.

When a nation loses its independence, one of two consequences must follow: either it is destroyed in the last struggle, or it is amalgamated with its conquerors. The nation may be preserved in its separate members; but in its collective form, its especial purpose, its nationality in fine, it exists no longer. To the existence of the Jewish race no such close was appointed, for the fulfilment of its lofty mission forbade alike its annihilation and its amalgamation with its conquerors. That race was dispersed, retaining in its dispersion its peculiar character. This dispersion was the instrument of its material salvation. Had this numerically insignificant nation remained in Palestine, it could not have retained its integrity amid the irruptions of the barbarians, the conquests of the Mahomedan Arabians, the incursions of Ghengis Khan and of the Saracens and Turcomans. That it had been conquered and dismembered by the tolerant Romans before the outbreak of these wars of devastation and of the Crusades, was a beneficent ordination of the Almighty Ruler of the Universe, and an evidence of His governing providence.

The existence of the Jewish race as a people was not necessary, says Dr. Philipson[*]. Indeed the accomplishment of their sacred task was far more powerfully aided by their dispersion. Through the absence of all political and municipal vitality in the numerous isolated communities, was this their task more promptly and efficiently performed. The religious idea was, by the dispersion of the Jews, freed from the trammelling influence of political and municipal life, and space and opportunity were secured to its depositaries for their own and its preservation.

---

[*] Die Entwickelung der religiösen Idee von Dr. Ludwig Philipson. Magdeburg, 1847.

But for this end, it was also necessary that the Jews should be placed in a position which would prevent their amalgamation with the dominant nation in whose centre they from time to time dwelt. On this point we are anxious to avoid misapprehension. We would, therefore, observe that we here refer exclusively to the times at which nations were specifically ruled by the two new Churches, in part antagonistic to the religious idea, viz., Christianity and Moslemism —then in their most dogmatic stage of development— an era at which the political amalgamation of the Hebrew race would have been inevitably combined with an absorption of the religious idea into the forms of Christianity and Islamism; an age, as will be admitted, wholly different in its character from the present time, and necessitating, consequently, wholly different conditions of existence.

That the Jewish race should assume in their dispersions a distinctive and isolating mental costume and character, which should place them in strong contrast to the dominant Churches, and that their temporal position should be exclusive in its tendency, so as to render them wholly dependent on themselves and their own resources, was a historical necessity. Both conditions were indispensable to the preservation of the Jewish race in its integrity, and both were fulfilled. It may be objected, and with truth, if the material fact be alone considered, that the social position of the Jews, and the oppression and suffering to which they were exposed, were virtually brought about by the peculiarities to which the race so pertinaciously adhered. But if the Jews had not, both from choice and necessity, preserved their individuality, their fusion with the other dominant creeds would have been inevitable; and true it certainly is, that had they forsaken Judaism, they would have had nothing to endure. The service of the *Religious Idea* rendered this immunity impossible. Nor does this afford to the dominant Churches the slightest justification for the tyranny and cruelty exercised by them towards the Hebrew race. The peculiarity of our fellow-man, as long as it does no injury to society, in no way gives us the right to injure him in life, property and honor; nor to beat him to death, either morally or physically. And the preservation of this peculiarity was the only reproach cast upon the Jews after they had been degraded to the very lowest social position by their oppressors. However, for this condition of things there existed a historical necessity. To the Jewish race it was given to preserve within itself the *Religious Idea*, unscathed by the antagonisms of the dominant Christian and Mahomedan Churches. The only means by which this could be carried out was the adoption of a peculiar external form of *religious life*. So soon as the dominant Churches came to comprehend the antagonisms to their own systems inherent in Judaism, they naturally sought to annihilate Judaism, or to thrust aside and supplant it. The necessary consequences of this animosity were the constant persecutions of the Jews, and their political and municipal expulsion, whether as communities or as individuals.

Another historical feature of the Middle Ages was the feudal system. Its most marked tendency was the subdivision of the State into guilds or companies. Feudalism split up the aggregate of society into many separate bodies, and assigned to each a particular position and constitution, and individual rights and privileges. Instead of erecting the State on the universal basis of equal and general rights; instead of comprehending each and every portion of society as constituting an integral part of the whole social fabric; instead of recognising the people collectively to be one body politic, feudalism divides and subdivides them, according to a certain fixed scheme, from the monarch down to the serf, into classes, guilds, corporations, and arranges them in orders, companies, &c., that stand to each other in the relative positions of inferior and superior.

What post was appointed to the Jew in this feudal state? What rank was he to hold in this scheme? Neither amid the nobles, nor the guilds of the towns, nor the serfdom of the peasant, would it concede a place to the Hebrew. Feudalism compelled the Jew to remain a foreign excrescence, an outcast from them all. By feudalism the Jews were considered to be but appendages of the monarch, who in his gracious clemency tolerated their presence as imperial or royal menials. They paid tribute to the sovereign, were under his immediate protection, which he could grant, or rather sell to them or withhold from them, at his royal pleasure. They were thus denied all rights, were compelled to dwell in separate quarters of the towns; were forbidden to hold land, and to pursue any trade. But one alternative was allowed, but one dark retreat afforded them, whence their fellow-men shrunk in disgust. Permission was accorded them to wander as hawkers, pedlars, and money-lenders, footsore and weary, from place to place. How true were then the poet's words:—

> "The wild dove hath her nest, the fox his cave,
> Mankind their country, Israel but the grave."

So abject was the plight to which the feudal system had reduced the sons of Israel—those who in Palestine had been a free and agricultural people; in Rome, Roman citizens—were now condemned to be hirelings and menials, earning their exiles' bread in the land of their birth by hawking and usury. Princes and emperors pledged their right to the tenure of Jews, sometimes to towns, sometimes to feudal lords of higher or lower degree. For other instances they conceded their claim to the servitude of the Jews for payment; or in compliance with petitions or threats, to certain districts and towns. From this arbitrary and lawless rule to which they were subjected, other and serious evils resulted to the Jews. The callings they were permitted to pursue acted prejudicially on their moral condition. It may with truth be asserted that the highest credit redounds to the Jewish race that under the pressure of circumstances so degrading, they not only were not wholly demoralised, but preserved a freshness of spirit and a strength of character which they mainly derived from the peculiar constitution of their spiritual and religious life. In other instances, again, these pursuits brought them constantly into collision with great and small. The borrower hates the lender; the more deeply he is indebted, the more entirely he is in the power of his creditor, and the more anxious is he to set him aside by physical force, particularly in an age when might made right, and when that lender was without arms and without legal defence. Thus the longer the Jews remained in any one locality, the more imminent and certain were their persecution and expulsion; simply because the number of those whose interest it was to effect their removal was greater.

A third and necessary consequence was, that just as the snail ever seeks shelter within its shelly tenement from the bruising heel of the passer-by, so the persecuted Jew ever withdrew deeper and deeper into intellectual seclusion. All spiritual connection with other nations gradually ceased. An attachment to scientific pursuits, which endured to a much later period among the Jews than among the Arabians and Christians, expired at length amid the universal persecutions to which they were subjected, particularly those which accompanied their expulsion from Spain. At the era when the taste for classical studies was revived, and when the other European peoples gladly shook off their long intellectual lethargy no ray of morning light could penetrate into the dark Ghetto, or Jews' quarter, and dawn on the mental vision of the crouching and hopefallen son of Abraham. Even religious speculation was arrested in the crushed spirits that were only permanently saved from entire paralysation by the exciting study of the Talmud whetting the edge of intellectual subtlety, though this was limited to the analytical disquisitions of casuistry. Of this the result is manifest; the ecclesiastical system of the Middle Ages sought, in its spirit of exclusiveness, to annihilate the Jews, since in Judaism was included the most uncompromising antagonism to that exclusiveness—the *Religious Idea*. Where they could not succeed in extirpating, they tried to expel them from municipal society. Feudalism, amid its divisions, and subdivisions, that virtually denied the equality of human rights, had no place for the outcast of the Church—the rejected Hebrews. It placed them without the pale of law and right, and as it transformed the peasantry into the bondmen of the nobles, so it made the Jews to be the bondmen of the monarch. Yet, as compared with the Church, the feudal system was the salvation of Judaism. From the personal influence of the monarch they often derived protection: seeing that, as occasion might be, the sovereigns either thought more tolerantly, or felt more humanely than the petty tyrants, their subjects; or they needed the gold of the Jews, their loans, the purchase-money of protection; or they were impelled to uphold them by a spirit of opposition to the Church, which spirit was not unfrequently rife in Christendom.

And the Jews, in truth, required nought, save according to the necessities of the hour, a few spots of earth on which to exist, to weather the storm, and to outlive the days of menaced extermination.

If we have now made clear the historical necessity for the position of the Jews in the Middle Ages, as also the conditions by which it was attained, let us proceed briefly to review the facts as they arose :—

After the final conflicts with the pagan Romans, the Jews had obtained the full rights of Roman citizenship, and during its enjoyment, gained a considerable degree of prosperity, and possessed entire civil and religious freedom, in so far as the former anywhere existed. The first Roman Emperors who adopted the Christian religion were compelled to exercise their rule tolerantly in their half-heathen, half-Christian dominions. So soon, however as the Christian Church obtained temporal sway, it began to oppose the Jews, even in their very existence. Bishops who were held to be shining lights among the Church Fathers, such as the holy Ambrosius, Cyril, and others, hurled anathemas and excited the populace against the Jews. Synagogues were reduced to ashes, whole communities compelled by means of murder and plunder to self-expatriation. The councils having found that the Jews were not to be won over to Christianity in the mass, zealously opposed all peaceful social intercourse with them. Marriages between Jews and Christians were interdicted; the Christians were forbidden even to eat with the Jew; the Jews to have Christian servants, while the Christians were allowed to employ Jews in this capacity. Under such influence, the emperors issued successive decrees, by which the municipal condition of the Jews became more and more fettered; they were expelled from the army, excluded from the civil service, and were at length deprived of all offices of honor in the municipalities, till, under the Emperors Honorius and Arcadius, in the year 430, they were wholly despoiled of all civil rights, and degraded to the very lowest class among the people. It is here worthy of special note, that these very decrees (preserved to us in the *Codex Theodosianus*) declare the Jews to be innocent, and thus testify that they were issued on religious grounds only. For these decrees, while successively depriving the Jews of one right after the other, contain consolatory and laudatory expressions, and refer to such remnants of civil liberty as were preserved, till the final stroke was put to this cruel spoliation. Thus the Church had deprived the Jews of all legal rights, had excluded them from all civil society, long before feudalism had come into existence.

When Moslemism subdued and overspread the Eastern world, it assumed, politically only, an attitude hostile to the Jews. Islamism sought but empire, and never practised religious persecution against the Israelites. When excluding the Jews from public functions (those connected with the financial administration excepted) and even when depriving them of privileges enjoyed by true believers, as their right, Mahomedanism granted to the Israelites religious toleration; but when the East early relapsed into a state of stagnation and non-progress, when the elements of despotism developed themselves more and more in Mahomedan rule, the Jews participated in this degeneracy, and became an ignorant, motionless, spiritless mass.

In Gaul and Spain, the Jews enjoyed under the Goths the full rights of citizenship. This rendered it the more natural that the Catholic Franks should regard them as adversaries, should deprive them of their legal immunities, and in obedience to the behests of the clergy, should interfere with the freedom of their religious worship, encroach upon their possessions, and coerce them to accept baptism. In Spain, therefore, the Jews hailed the advent of the Moors as that of deliverers, who ensured to them renewed security and peace.

In the extensive dominions of Charles the Great, at the time when feudalism began to prevail, the Jews were of infinite service in the State. Their frequent journeys, their wide-spreading connections, their acquaintance with all parts of the empire, their dexterity, tact and activity, singularly qualified them for the performance of business of various kinds; in circumstances, too, where the ignorance of the great, and even of the ecclesiastics, and the abject condition of the people, would have given rise to considerable embarrassment. On these accounts, favor was shown them; permission to hold landed property, and protection against encroachment and oppression were granted them. The weaker, however, the royal rule of Charles' and Louis' successors became, the more enmity the clergy and councils showed towards the Jews; the more the feudal system developed itself, the deeper sank the Jewish race; demands upon them for money became more and more numerous; taxes on beds, parchments and kitchens, taxes for comings-in and goings-out, followed in rapid succession, and formed at least one source of the interest entertained by the monarch in the presence of Jews in his dominions. Scarcely, however, had the feudal system assigned to the Israelites a position which, though denying them all rights, was yet determined by law, when the Church, to whose power the Crusades had given a fresh impulse, reintroduced in an extended form the persecution of the Jews throughout Europe. The first outbreak of the Crusades reached the Jews, and the flames spread from its birthplace, Treves, over the whole empire. Metz, Cologne, Worms, Mayence, Speyer, prepared destruction and death to the proscribed sons of Israel. They fled to Moravia, Silesia and Poland. After the close of the Crusades, the revival of the accusations against them of purloining the host and of drinking the blood of Christian children, excited the people to frenzy and to deeds of blood, and thousands of Jews without distinction of age or sex, were mercilessly sacrificed. The carnage began on this occasion in Switzerland and extended to the borders of Poland. These abominations did not cease till the years of the Reformation; and even then were occasionally revived; while in their social position they were even the more enslaved; they were denied all connection with human society, they were excluded from all participation in the world's movements. They paid tribute for their very bodies, like the beasts of the field.

While often exposed to murderous violence on the blood-stained soil of Germany, but allowed to exist as a race, they were repeatedly expelled from Spain, France, and England. From Spain, where under the Moorish rule the Jews had attained a high, social, literary and scientific position, they were in the year 1492 wholly expelled by Ferdinand, the expeller of the Moors. Three hundred thousand left their beautiful fatherland; of these, some perished by the way, others fled to Barbary, and others sought refuge in Turkey and Holland. Four times were the Jews banished from France, and as frequently recalled. In 1299, they were driven from England, where they had long dwelt, but where their exclusion from all save financial business had especially exposed them to the exactions of petty sovereigns. In the time of Cromwell they were re-admitted into Great Britain. After the successful struggle in the Netherlands, against the tyranny of Philip II., they found a ready asylum in that country, and from the commencement a recognition of their freedom and rights.

We thus perceive that, until the close of the last century, the Jews remained wholly excluded from municipal society, lived in separate quarters of the town, were interdicted from holding land, from exercising certain trades and callings, from pursuing agriculture, from entering into commercial pursuits, and from adopting the vocation of teachers. They were further excluded from the civil and municipal services of the State, and were thus forced to the exclusive assumption of the callings of money-lenders, hawkers and pedlars, as the sole means by which to exist; and even in these, they were subjected to enormous taxes, and to the payment of protection-money and head-money. It may be truly said with respect to their moral treatment, that they were everywhere exposed to contempt and hatred, everywhere despised and oppressed. Forbidden to approach the academies, whether of science or art, shut out from intellectual communion with the rest of the family of man—they were thus, for mental food, cast upon the pages of the Talmud alone. By a singular accident, the faculty of medicine formed the sole exception to this wholesale prohibition.

Yet, notwithstanding all this, notwithstanding the fearful passage through fifteen hundred years of misery, strong elements of life were latent in the bosom of Judaism. The first of these was their inflexible fidelity to the *Religious Idea*, and its elaboration in Talmudism, which fidelity neither the horror of death, nor the martyrdom of contempt and scorn, nor the snare of the tempter was of power to shake. The Jews everywhere saw close at hand the boundary line over which, if they passed, sorrow and suffering were left behind, viz., their passage to Christianity or to Mahomedanism; but over that boundary they passed not. And this fidelity was not the appanage of the chosen few, of the best spirits among them, but of the mass; of the last, as of the first members of their race. Besides this, they found within their own communities, cities of refuge to which to flee, which offered them protection from the infliction of outward injustice and maltreatment. Congregational life never ceased from the midst of them. Wherever ten Jews were assembled in one locality, they formed themselves into a congregation, as though they had been dwelling upon the free soil of Palestine; a congregation whose fundamental principles were everywhere personal equality, free choice of their officials, in which dwelt not a trace of the custom of life-tenure or hereditary succession; a distinct, yet powerful echo of the voice of Mosaism. Within such congregations, the synagogue and its service were the first objects of care; then charitable institutions for the relief of the sick, the indigent, the old and the imprisoned; for poor brides, for the dying, and for the interment of the dead. The next meteors of solicitude were the schools, some destined for the instruction of youth, others of adults, in which the subjects taught were naturally restricted to the domain of Talmudic and Rabbinical learning. In this congregational life the Jews found not only inexhaustible sources of indemnification for external evils and some means to avert them, but also partial compensation for their exclusion from all participation in general and political existence.

A second shelter the Jew found in the sanctuary of domestic or family life. Repulsed from without, man seeks consolation in the arms of those dear ones belonging to him. The threshold of his house is the boundary-stone beyond which scorn and contumely cannot pass. Within, he finds the love, esteem, and reverence denied him without. Among the Jews unbounded was the intensity of family ties and affections. The bond between parent and child, and the conjugal relation, were alike sacred and exalted, prompting to efforts and sacrifices the most sublime. The exclusion from society, and the binding Talmudic statute, necessarily co-operated to keep the Jews removed and free from the great vices of the age. On the one hand, temperance and chastity disinclining them to excess; on the other, an entire indisposition to deeds of murder, rapine, violence, brutality, and combativeness, were deep-seated qualities in the Jewish heart. If in respect of property they evinced less conscientiousness, so that they were too often prone to artifice, deceit and over-reaching; to the circumstances of their enforced condition may this be with justice imputed, while they ever abhorred to raise their hands against the lives of their fellow-beings, and never abandoned themselves to profligacy and sensuality.

All this in combination, rendered possible and effected the preservation of the Jewish race during the seventeen centuries of direst persecution, through which, after the destruction of Jerusalem, they struggled as for existence, till a new time dawned upon them at the commencement of the present century. The position of isolation, exclusion, and repudiation, in which ever dwelt this race, rendered its amalgamation with other peoples impossible —the Religious Idea, of which the Jewish mind held tenacious possession, whose truth had permeated the very being of this race from its first to its last member, and endowed it with resistless force and was its isolating peculiarity—the distinctive character imprinted by Talmudism on daily existence—the acuteness of intellect developed and kept alive in the whole mass by Talmudic studies—congregational life—the depth and strength of family ties and affections—the freedom from the coarsest vices and from moral depravity—all these were, we repeat, the elements which, in combination, invested the Jewish body-politic with a resisting power that enabled them to repel and defy the forces external to themselves aiming at their annihilation. Thus the Jews furnish historical proof that, not only an individual man, but whole races of men, so soon as they have truth dwelling in them, cannot be subdued by any power, whether of Church or State—by any oppression, however stringent and enduring. Judaism existed not only during the whole of the Middle Ages—Judaism not only outlived the dominion of the Roman—Judaism not only witnessed the fall of all peoples of antiquity, the migrations of countless races, and the irruptions of new ones—it survived not only the rise of Christianity and Moslemism, but it still lives on to behold the dawn of a new era, the development of new social and religious mutations. It has done yet more. With this new era it was itself born to new life; an era when Judaism and the Jews have stepped forth from their isolation and exclusion into the general world of man.

Thus the great import of these fifteen hundred years is this. The Christian Church sought to annihilate the Jews, and with them the antagonism to itself, of which they are the depositaries. Being unable in consequence of the dispersion, to accomplish its aim, it condemned the Jews to unmerited exclusion, of which the Roman emperors and the feudal system were the successive instruments. But the Jews overcame all obstacles to their continued existence, adhered within Talmudism to the religious idea, and arose at the dawn of a new era, towards the close of the last century, to re-enter in every relation of life the general world of man.

History, like her eternal sister Nature, possesses the great privilege of recording the general results of events, and of passing silently over the griefs and sufferings laid successively by individuals on the altar of the general good. The uninterrupted and eternal production of life is the law of nature. But life necessitates death. Countless old generations must die that countless new generations may be born. In order to sustain life nature must destroy life. In like manner, history requires the suffering and the annihilation of millions of individual men, in order to secure to the race of man continued and progressive development, and to prepare for it an ever greater future, an ever more glorious existence. Judged according to this standard, the thousand holocausts which the annals of every people record are recognised to have been offered for a loftier end. History, which would otherwise present a melancholy picture of tyranny and slavery, of force and thraldom, of human sufferings and passions, becomes, when viewed in this light, a solemn record of the eternal strivings of mankind for higher objects, of its aspirations for the conquest of truth and right.

Let us thus look upon the history of the Jews in their dispersions, and we shall at once perceive that these dispersions had for aim and end the preservation of the Religious Idea; and that all that the Jews, its depositaries and bearers, were called upon to endure all their sufferings during fifteen centuries (of which sufferings alas! many still continue) were a necessity which in the fulfil' ment of their sublime mission could not be averted. Nay, instead of the remembrance of the evil treatment received by this peaceable people causing us to mourn, the thought should rather inspire us with feelings of admiration at the inward power of the spirit, enabling a whole race to conquer all disasters and defy al₁ calamities. What more does Judaism desire? It has gained the victory. The world sought to annihilate it, and yet Judaism exists. The world strove to render it dumb, and Judaism speaks, speaks now, even louder and more audibly than ever, in the ears of mankind. Yet more—Judaism sees the animosity which prevailed against her daily diminish—hears the world rescind daily its hostile edicts—feels her sufferings and anguish pass away, virulence and oppression gradually die out. Judaism may with truth exclaim, 'I have endured to the end; and this endurance has won its reward.' It has achieved that which it was its task to accomplish; it has preserved the *Religious Idea* for the great future of mankind. Let us, therefore, not deem the history of the Jews in their dispersions to be but a blood-stained record of uniform oppression and violence. Let us, on the contrary, recognise it to be that which it truly is—the conflict of the Spirit with its antagonisms for the eternal preservation of the *Religious Idea*. Seen under this aspect, the existence of the Jewish people is neither a mystic riddle, as by some it has been supposed to be, for the key to its solution lies at hand; nor is it a mournful picture veiled in sadness; it is a brilliant image, delineating the power of the immortal soul of man.

JUDAISM IN AUSTRALIA.

Far away from the centres of Judaism in the Old World, removed by leagues of land and sea, by change of climate, thought and habit from the "Home," the flame of Judaism yet burns brightly in Australia. As in ancient days, the exiles carried fire from their altars to the strange land whither they went forth to dwell—so do the Jews of the present, whithersoever they wander, carry with them the fire of Judaism, to burn on the new altars which they have raised in their wanderings. Yes, even in this "Ultima Thule," this remote region, where the Jew must turn westward rather than eastward if he would look towards Jerusalem; where Passover is in the autumn, and the Feast of Tabernacles in the spring of the year: still pious eyes are lifted towards the Holy Home, and pious hearts beat for the Restoration.

First Jewish Worship in 1839.

The commencement of the celebration of the rites and ordinances of the Jewish faith in Melbourne was a singularly modest one, and dates far back in the annals of the colony. Even as the Israelites of old in the wilderness had to content themselves with a tabernacle as their place of worship, so their descendants in this far Southern land erected their tent in the then almost wilderness for the worship of the Most High in accordance with all their ancient usages and traditions. Divine service was held for the first time in Melbourne on the festival of the year 5600—1839, at the house of Mr. M. Lazarus, Collins-street west. The Jewish residents then residing in this city were not sufficient in number to form a *Minyan*. In fact, at this gathering the chief persons who took an interest in Judaism were Messrs. Solomon Benjamin and Michael Cashmore. This gathering of Israel in the wilderness was shortly reinforced by the arrival in the colony of Messrs. Edward and Isaac Hart. Mr. Edward Hart was gifted with a naturally sweet and pleasant voice, and had an aptitude for *Chasonoth* which fitted him particularly for the services which he gladly rendered. Divine service was held on the New Year Festivals 1840, at the residence of Mr. Solomon Benjamin, and the prayers were read on that occasion by Messrs. Edward Hart, Michael Cashmore, S. H. Harris, and Isaac Lincoln. This was the first service held in Melbourne with a full *Minyan*. And to the Harts, the Benjamins, and Mr. M. Cashmore is due the honor of transplanting Judaism to this colony, and of fostering and aiding the youthful Synagogue in its early struggles. To these and others, who in the early days, under many and great difficulties, bore the burden and heat of the day, and devoted time, wealth, influence and energy to the maintenance and spread of their religion, the Jews of the present day cannot be too grateful. Now that the work is virtually accomplished, the whole system of Judaism firmly established in good working order, with its whole apparatus of schools, alms-houses, charitable institutions, &c., &c., the impartial historian in reviewing the facts connected with the early history of the Synagogue in Victoria cannot fail to be struck with the zeal and earnestness displayed by these devoted men.

THE LATE ASHER HYMEN HART.

Conspicuous among the honored names of that period is that of the late Asher Hymen Hart, who must be regarded as the chief and real pioneer who cleared the way and acclimatised the practices and ordinances of the Jewish religion in this colony. He not only gave time and means in aid of the congregation, but also acted for many years himself in the capacity of honorary lay reader, and performed the functions of a minister, until the services of a duly authorised and properly-qualified Rabbi could be secured. That gentleman, embued with true love for his nation and devotion to his religion which have characterised the whole course of his life, made it his first care, as soon as he had set foot in Melbourne, to enquire of his co-religionists—" What have you done towards establishing a congregation and a permanent place of worship"; and when he found that there was no organised community and no synagogue, his first endeavors were directed towards the establishing of Judaism in this city on a sound basis, and to erect a place of worship to the Most High. Diligently did he set to work to carry out his resolutions and to accomplish the work he had set before himself. Being a man of extensive reading and superior natural ability, he at once took the lead of his co-religionists, and succeeded in inaugurating a new era for Judaism in Victoria. In 1841, therefore, we find Mr. Hart already conducting Divine worship in an able and systematic manner. The New Year and *Yom Kipur* services in 1841 were held at the (then unoccupied) Port Phillip Hotel, Flinders-street. The number of attendants was about 25. Mr. A. H. Hart was on that occasion assisted by Messrs. Isaac Lincoln, E. Hart, and Lewis Nathan; the latter gentleman (one of the present Board of Deputies, London) being on a visit to this colony from Hobart Town, Tasmania.

A POOR SOCIETY ESTABLISHED.

Shortly before Mr. A. H. Hart's arrival in Melbourne a society had been established among the Jewish residents for the purpose of assisting their indigent co-religionists. This institution, however, had but a short existence, for Mr. Hart, at a meeting which on his personal invitation was held at the residence of Messrs. Ed. and Isaac Hart, pointed out to the Jewish residents of Melbourne that the natural feeling of sympathy which existed between a Jew and his brother would supply all that was needed. He contended that the natural tie of Jew and Jew was strong enough without requiring any formal pledge to assist one another. And if any poor brother found his way to Melbourne from the neighboring colonies, he would find friends to assist him. The want of bodily food to the Australian Jew was not to be compared to the want of spiritual food. In the one case the remedy was at hand in the charitable spirit of every true disciple of Moses; but the other want—the spiritual—was one which could only be supplied by constant and persistent effort: a permanent place of worship was the great want to be supplied. Mr. Hart's eloquence and earnestness produced the desired effect, since the spark to kindle the latent fire of Judaism within being all that was required from his hearers. Those present at once agreed to alter the constitution of the society, as recommended by Mr. A. H. Hart. In 1844 a site of land was procured from the Government by Messrs. A. H. Hart, M. Cashmore, and Solomon Benjamin, and as soon as a sufficient sum of money was accumulated, a very suitable building was erected. The foundation-stone of this synagogue was laid by Mr. Solomon Benjamin. From 1841 until the first synagogue was opened, divine worship was held at the residence of Mr. Benjamin.

The First Jewish Burial in Victoria.

Not only in the direction of synagogue matters was Mr. A. H. Hart's influences beneficially exerted but also in many other ways. The case of a Jewish girl named Davies, who was buried before Mr. Hart's arrival in the colony, in unconsecrated ground near the Merri Creek, awakened his ever active sympathies, and through his exertions the Jews obtained a grant of land in the Old Cemetery. Sad to say, the first participant in this melancholy privilege of being buried in consecrated ground was Mr Lewis Hart, a brother of the gentleman whose career of usefulness we have faintly indicated, who died suddenly, after a few months' residence in the colony. In this case the sad duties and services due to the departed were rendered by Mr. A. H. Hart himself. A tombstone erected to the memory of the deceased yet bears the first Hebrew inscription which was written by the hand of the bereaved brother.

Foundation Stone of the Present Synagogue Laid 1853.

In 1853 the present Synagogue was built and the children of Abraham met in Victoria for the worship of the Most High, in a place befitting their high aims and aspirations, and which reflected credit both on their energy and liberality. The foundation stone of this building was laid by the indefatigable, zealous, and liberal Mr. David Benjamin (now in London) on the 1st of

December in the above-mentioned year, and his name is commemorated on a memorial tablet, which will be observed by the visitor on the right of the entrance.

INTERIOR OF THE SYNAGOGUE DECORATED, 1858.

For four years the interior of the Synagogue remained unfinished, and the ceremony, in consequence of the complete repair and decoration, took place on September 2nd, 1858. The consecration service was conducted by the Rev. E. M. Myers (now in Montreal), assisted by Messrs. S. Phillips, secretary, S. Nelson, conductor of the choir, and Michael Cashmore, president of the congregation. More than a thousand persons were present, and conspicuous amidst the congregation was Rabbi Cohen, of Jerusalem, who came to the colony for the purpose of collecting subscriptions for the relief of the distressed Jews in Palestine. To his long flowing robes and Turkish turban the Rabbi realised pretty nearly the representation of the High Priest of the Jews in days gone by.

PALMAM QUI MERUIT FERAT.

The Benjamins have always been among the best supporters of Judaism in this city, and their names are honorably associated with every enterprise connected with religious teaching or observance.

In looking at the list of donations to the present Synagogue we find it headed by David Benjamin, Esq., who munificently gave £1000, and Moses Benjamin, Esq., J.P., by £500.

There are many other Jews who also acted nobly and supported the cause of their religion in the metropolis of the South, such as the late Hon. Edward Cohen, M.L.A., the late Mr. Henry Harris, and others, gentlemen whose names stand high before the world, not only as staunch supporters of their ancient creed, but also as liberal active supporters of every charitable and benevolent movement, with a noble freedom from prejudice; men who observe not only the letter but also the spirit of the Law, and who thereby have gained the admiration of every class of their fellow-citizens. But to mention the names of all who have taken an interest in Synagogal matters would be too great a task, and quite beyond the limit of this sketch. All that concerns us at

---

No notice has been taken in the present work of that distinguished and self-denying body of men who have associated themselves in other ways with the spread and the teaching of Judaical Truth, and the establishment of the apparatus of schools, benevolent institutions, and charitable missions, which has so long and eminently characterised the chosen people. Had this been done, it would have tended to swell the work beyond the limit within which it was necessary to confine it. Such men as Mr. Moses Goldstein, whose liberality and kindness of heart, coupled with the self-sacrificing and assiduous manner in which for years he has discharged the arduous duties of hon. director of funerals has gained him universal respect and esteem. Mr. Solomon Joseph, the founder of the

present is to state a few facts in connection with the establishment of the congregation, and to report the proceedings at the consecration of the renovation of the synagogue, which took place on Sunday, the 26th of August, 1877, under the direction of Lewis M. Myers, Esq, the President for the present year, and Past Treasurer, who has taken a lively interest and active part in the work in question, and in the progress and promotion of the interests, aims, and objects of Judaism generally.

DESCRIPTION OF
בית הכנסת דק׳ק שארית ישראל

The Synagogue is situated in Bourke-street west, and on the brow of the hill. It is approached by a flight of bluestone steps, leading to a portico in the Italian style, occupying the whole front of the building, supported by six columns of the Composite order, and supported by a well-proportioned pediment. Over the entrance-door is a tablet setting forth the date of foundation, and the name of the congregation in Hebrew. Wide swing doors lead into the Synagogue, the total length of which is 70 feet, and the extreme width is 40 feet; the height from floor to ceiling is about 30 feet; this latter is coffered and richly decorated, gilt pendants hang from the intersections. A ladies' gallery spans three sides of the building, supported by fluted columns, with foliated caps and carved brackets. At the northern end of the Synagogue is the היכל (ark); this consists of two large columns, one on each side, the shafts of which are painted to resemble Sienna marble, with richly foliated caps, the whole bearing a highly-enriched cornice, on which are inscribed in Hebrew the words " Know before Whom thou standest"; the columns are backed by pilasters, and the central portion filled by an arch richly moulded with flowers, fruits, etc., the opening of which is covered by polished mahogany doors and a heavy velvet curtain; two triple lamps, one on each side, shed their rays over the whole, and a perpetual lamp hangs from the centre; an ornamented tablet on the top of the cornice, with the decalogue in Hebrew thereon, and a flight of marble steps below, complete the *tout ensemble*. Two tablets with a prayer for the Royal family, in Hebrew and English respectively on them, hang on each side of the ark. In the centre of the building is the בימה (reading desk) and choir, which is panelled and decorated with fruits and flowers, richly gilded.

Jewish press in the colonies, would also not go unnoticed, for although the Australian Jews do not now possess an organ of their own, yet the foundation has been laid by that gentleman for its proper establishment, and for the promotion of this most important means of furthering the ends and aims and inculcating a correct understanding of the tenets and truths of Judaism. However, in a future publication now in course of preparation ("*Jews and Judaism in the Antipodes*") these omissions will be fully supplied, and an exhaustive record of the progress of Judaism in all its phases up to the present time furnished.

Sittings to the number of 402 run down the east, west and south sides of the building, and 250 in the gallery, which are of carved cedar, highly polished. Light is diffused through the Synagogue by means of large windows glazed with frosted glass, with yellow and ruby color stained glass borders alternately. Attached to the Synagogue is a robingroom for ministers and choir, vestry room, succah, etc. The original cost of the Synagogue was £11500, and that of the renovation £2,500. A collection was made after the ceremony had been gone through, and the sum of £500 subscribed, Moses Benjamin, Esq., J.P., being a contributor of £100.

THE CONSECRATION IN 1877.

The ceremony of the consecration of this Synagogue, on the occasion of its re-opening, took place on Sunday, 26th August, in the afternoon, at three o'clock. There was a crowded congregation, the body of the building being filled with gentlemen, amongst whom were a large number of Christians, the Rev. Thomas Jones, the Poet preacher, and Rev Charles Strong, being present. The ceremony commenced by the ministers and officers of the several congregations in the colony bringing the scrolls of the law to the door of the Synagogue. Each scroll was inclosed in a velvet case, richly and variously ornamented. The officiating ministers were the Rev. Dr. Dättner Jacobson, Melbourne Hebrew congregation; Rev. Raphael Benjamin, B.A., Melbourne Hebrew congregation; Rev. Samuel Herman, Hebrew congregation, Geelong; Rev Moses Rintel, East Melbourne Hebrew congregation; Rev. Elias Blaubaum, Hebrew congregation. St. Kilda; Rev. J. M. Goldreich, Hebrew congregation, Ballarat.* The congregation having taken their seats, the officiating ministers, followed by the wardens of the Synagogue, brought the scrolls of the law (24 in number) to the door of the building, and the leading minister said—

"Open unto me the gates of righteousness;
I will enter them, and praise the Lord."

The doors were then opened, and the procession, consisting of the ministers and chief officers of the different congregations, entered, each carrying a scroll. The procession having arrived at the ark, commenced to seven times circuit the Synagogue. During each circuit a psalm was chanted, and at the end of each chant, while the leading minister stood under a canopy in front of the ark, the choir sang the following verse:— §

"Thanks to thee, O Lord, we render,
Let Thy grace accept our lay;
Words are all we now can tender,
All the homage man can pay."

---

* The Rev. Mr. Stone, of the Sandhurst Hebrew Congregation, was absent through indisposition.

§ The Rev. Raphael Benjamin's adaptation of a passage from Handel's *Judas Maccabæus*.

The seven circuits having been made, the procession approached the ark. The heavy velvet curtain was withdrawn, the doors were rolled back, and the scrolls of the law placed within. The Rev. Mr. Benjamin then commenced the usual afternoon service, and after it was gone through, the Rev. Dr. Dättner Jacobson delivered an address.

The Rev. Dr. Dattner Jacobson.

Although the leading tenets and principles of the religion of the Hebrews are so simple and so easily learnt as not to require any vast erudition to teach rudimentarily, and in a certain sense every good Jew may be said to be his own priest; yet this is by no means a satisfactory or desirable situation for the Synagogue. In times past the progress of Judaism has been slow, and its followers devoted and zealous, as they undoubtedly are, have labored under many and depressing disadvantages from the want of competent instructors. Looking back upon the past, the road is only now and again speckled with a few green and cheering oases, in times when a revival of religious feeling and enthusiasm has taken place; but since the departure of the Rev. A. F. Ornstein the Melbourne Hebrew congregation has been without an actual head. Since then the services have been carried on and the duties devolving upon the head were performed by the Rev. Raphael Benjamin, B.A., who though originally engaged as Teacher and Second Reader, yet when called upon to perform more serious and important functions, supplied the want and discharged his new and arduous duties in a manner which reflected the greatest credit upon himself, and gave unbounded satisfaction to the members of the congregation. Despite this gentleman's exertions, however, the want of a qualified and competent head was felt, and the appointment of the Rev. Dr. D. Jacobson was hailed with heartfelt satisfaction. Under his able leadership it is hoped that a new era of usefulness and revival is opening for the professors of the Hebrew faith in Melbourne, and that the beneficial influence of that gentleman's presence will be felt throughout the colony. This gentleman comes to Melbourne with University diplomas and testimonials from some of the leading Jews in Europe, which speak in the highest terms of his abilities and attainments. To speak of his erudition and accomplishments would be to assume the character of a panegyrist, and therefore we simply publish the sermon which he delivered on the occasion of the consecration of the Synagogue above referred to, without any comment on our own account. As for the rev. and learned Doctor's powers of oratory, none of those who were present on the occasion entertained any doubt, and but one opinion could be entertained, while the opinions of the daily press, which we extract, were of the most flattering kind. Little doubt exists but that Dr. Jacobson is a born orator, and that if after but two months' study of English, he was able to deliver such an address as that of the 26th, sure yet greater things may be confidently expected.

THE SERMON.
(Verbatim Report.)

Hail, sacred temple, with thy holy precincts! Ye rolls of the law, mercy seat, and pulpit, I salute you, in the name of Him who said "Let there be light." I salute you, also, honorable congregation, who have come here to worship and to glorify your God.

Dear friends, when I consider the great importance of the subject of my present discourse, and reflect upon the fact that, as regards the use of your beautiful language every one of this respectable assembly, compared with myself, is like a giant to a dwarf, or as a cedar-tree to a little insignificant plant. Verily, I must exclaim, as the great Moses did to God, בי ארני O Lord, my God, לא איש דברים אנכי. I am not a man of eloquence, כי כבד פה וכבד לשון אנכי for I am slow of speech, and of a slow tongue. By no means, dear brethren, do I stand here now to make a display of my rhetoric, and much less to boast of my knowledge, which is not more than a tiny drop out of the boundless ocean. But the deep importance of the subject, and my assurance of your kind indulgence inspire me with courage and confidence, and induce me to believe that though my speech be faulty, you, dear friends, will be able to understand me, even as the Lord answered Moses, מי שם פה לאדם. Cease, Moses, from thy complaining. Who made man's mouth? It is the Lord God, I say, whom we are all assembled here to worship and adore. Therefore, I fear not, and I am not discouraged to salute this holy re-decorated house. למען אחי ורעי אדברה נא שלום בך. On behalf of my brethren and friends, sacred temple, I render thee my salutations. למען בית אלהינו אבקשה טוב לך. On behalf of the Lord God I offer thee greeting.

מה טובו אהליך יעקב exclaims Balaam in Scripture, whilst praising Israel. How lovely are thy tents, O Jacob! משכנותיך ישראל and thy tabernacles, O Israel. כאהלים נטע ד'. Like the trees of lignaloes planted by God—כארזים על נחלי מים—as cedar trees beside the waters. This image, my friends, although it was depicted fully three thousand years ago, proves itself to be a most exact one again in our own days. For as the lign-aloe and the cedar are conspicuous for their perfect beauty, so is Israel now distinguished for perfect beauty in all its forms of worship.

זה אלי ואנוהו is Israel's watchword. This is my God, in whom is centred all beauty. הוד והדר לבושו. His garment—namely, the great universe, is the expression of the most perfect beauty.

ואת העיר שאמרו כלילת יופי. His chosen capital, Jerusalem, was called "complete beauty"—הנך יפה דודי אף נעים. Says the Synagogue to her God, "Oh, how beautiful art thou, my Beloved!

How I discern in *Thee* the highest ideal of the most perfect beauty! The heavy oppression of our forefathers, which weighed down upon them during the last centuries, dulled in them in some measure the delicate taste for beauty which at all times was proper to Israel. But the Israelite of the present day is beginning, by the free development of his power, once more to acknowledge, in the sphere of his religion, the claims of the Beautiful, and especially in his places of worship. What beautiful and magnificent Synagogues have been, during the last century, erected [in Israel! What holy emulation has animated men and women to adorn the places of devotion, the rolls of the law, the ark, the reading-desk, and the pulpit! Yes, yes, we must confess that since the destruction of the Temple in Jerusalem, and the Synagogue in Alexandria, Israel scarcely ever had Synagogues so exquisitely majestic, so heart-refreshing, and tending to inspire us with devotion, as at the present day.

כאהלים נטע ד'. The Judaism of the present, which, like the lign-aloe trees and cedars, distinguishes itself by a strong and powerful stem, knows how to stand up manly and seriously when it has to maintain its place and position. This Judaism—namely of the present day—has nothing to hide and nothing to conceal. The gates of its beautiful Synagogues it can open widely, and call everybody that passes by outside that he should only enter. Here, Judaism exclaims, lie my prayer-books, in Hebrew, English, and German! Read only the hymns which we have this day sung out of them.

מקימי מעפר דל. God raiseth up the poor from the dust, and also poor Israel from his oppression. הארץ נתן לבני אדם. "The earth God gave to mankind," nor has he excluded Israel from the right of possessing it. לא המתים יהללויה. The dead cannot praise God, that is, according to the explanation of the Talmud. לולב היבש פסול Dry and withered palms must not be used. שנאמר לא המתים יהללויה Because religion ought not to consist of dead and chilling formulas and ceremonies, but must be full of life and perennial freshness.

See here, dear visitors, these silver-adorned rolls which we carry about and kiss in our Synagogues, is our Thora. Do you know what is written therein? ואהבת לרעך כמוך is written in it—"Love thy neighbour as thyself." Come to our dwelling-places, to our homes, there also you will find written on the door-posts, ואהבת—"*Love and Friendship.*" Come to us every morning when we put the phylacteries on our hands and heads. There, *too*, you will find written ואהבה—"*Love and Friendship.*" Yes, indeed, we heartily rejoice at this command, and we would still more rejoice if *you* also would take this command to heart when dealing with us. This is our pulpit, which, notwithstanding its small space, has nevertheless room enough for the salvation of all nations that are susceptible of the feeling of *Love and Humanity.*

כארזים עלי מים. Yes, Judaism of the present is not the less to be compared to the lign-aloes and cedars, which are distinguished for their fragrance and refreshing shade.

Our ancestors in Germany and Poland have bequeathed to us a sad inheritance. They occupied themselves very little with that which was written outside of their narrow circle. It very seldom happened that Jews learnt the languages in which the masterpieces of literature were written, and scarcely were they able to express their ideas in intelligible language; the consequence of which was that during many centuries a literature was spread which heaped on the Jewish name hatred and scorn, without even one Jew being found who could take up his pen and refute the calumnies hurled at them by the defamers of their name.

But the Judaism of the present day, which has learned the languages of the nations, *was*, and *is*, in a position to enter on a war with the pen; to defend it victoriously, and make it honored and respected.

Now, should it be asked what have the Jews done to further the welfare of humanity at large? With what discoveries or inventions have they distinguished themselves? To that question the Judaism of the present would reply: For 1800 years I have been a witness to the whole world that religion may develop itself and exist without the support of the sword and State!

Listen! From a pulpit in the French capital, about 28 years ago, one of the most celebrated non-Jewish preachers—the great Lacordaire—in addressing his audience, spoke of the Jews. He did not speak of their cunning, nor of their duplicity. No, just the reverse. He proved to his hearers that the Jewish people is the most wonderful, social, and religious creation of antiquity. "Do you wish to have a conception of the gigantic structure of the Mosaic law," he exclaimed, "just recall to your memory, you sons of France, how many times even within the last half century you have altered your laws; and if you require another proof of the durability of the Mosaic code, you will find that proof in the Jews of the present day. For 1800 years Israel existed without a ruler, without a Temple, without a country, merely by force of their religious ideas."

"Do you not see," he again exclaimed, "that Israel defies the whole world; that of all the other nations, Israel alone has an existence of 4000 years, without there being as yet the slightest indication of a dissolution. Try and dig Israel the deepest of graves; immure it as securely as you wish, and place sentinels round about that grave, smilingly will Israel rise again, and prove to you that all material efforts are powerless against the spirit."

Again, accompany me to the capital of the Netherlands, and I will show another witness, says the Judaism of the present. There also preached, 150 years ago, one of your renowned ministers —the eloquent Saurin—the subject of his sermon being *Charity*.

We are told that his words made such a powerful impression on his audience that before they had left the church they gave all their valuables which they had with them away to the poor.

But the question is, by what means did that preacher produce such an effect on his hearers? By what means? Through no other but the description of the Jewish mode of giving charity. He described to them how the Jews of old gave their firstlings, their tithes, and sacrifices. He also enumerated the countless Jewish injunctions relating to sympathy for the poor, for strangers, widows and orphans. He also laid stress on the fact that at the present day, even in the smallest Jewish community, there is a charitable society for the purpose of assisting the poor, to which society every Jew contributes according to his means. This description of Jewish benevolence, which is worthy of emulation, acted as powerfully on his own audience as it did on the whole family of European nations, and helped to elevate their moral sentiment.

Your benevolent institutions, and the congregation here assembled to-day, also bear witness to the whole world how dear and sacred to you is the honor of Israel and that of his God. Who would not conscientiously acknowledge at the first sight of this sacred edifice that you are the rightful and unmistakable descendants of the Patriarch Jacob, who when turned away from the house of his father, and left without any worldly possessions, nevertheless said to his Maker, אם יהיה אלהים עמדי ? With thy assistance, O God, ונתן לי לחם לאכול ובגד ללבוש if Thou only grant me bread to eat and raiment to wear כל אשר תתן לי עשר אעשרנו לך I will even from this scanty allowance devote a tenth part to Thy holy service.

So, also, *you* descendants of the Patriarch Jacob—which of you enjoys the dew of heaven? Which of you lives upon the fat of the land? Which of you has not to earn his livelihood and the necessities of his household with the sweat of his brow? And yet, as soon as your contributions were required for religious purposes, to build and renovate the outward and visible sign of Judaism, nobody complained of want of means, and everything required was given richly and in abundance. כל אשר תתן לי עשר אעשרנו לך. Yes, to adorn Thy Temple, O Lord, I willingly give a portion even of my scanty means, and devote it to Thee with heartfelt joy.

Allow me, therefore, dear friends, to be on this occasion the representative of your religious feelings, like the firstlings placed into the hands of the priest, to offer to our God with filial gratitude your deep devotion, and to pray for his gracious acceptance.

Heavenly Father, receive the fervent words of thanks which come from the depths of the hearts of this congregation. אתה נהת ביד עבדך את התשועה הגדולה הזאת is the unanimous confession. Thy merciful assistance alone have we to thank for the completion of this our work. To Thy honor have we renovated this Temple, and to Thee we also consecrate it to-day, wherein Thy glory shall henceforth be praised. To Thee we consecrate all that is comprised within these walls. To Thee we consecrate the rolls of the Law, and may the word of life contained in them, penetrate all our hearts, and remain a faithful guide and companion throughout our whole life. To Thee we consecrate this pulpit from which Thy word shall re-echo and take deep root in our souls. To Thee we consecrate the נר תמיד, the perpetual burning lamp, emblem of Thy soul-warming religious flame, which by degrees must thaw and break up ice-cold religious opinions. And to Thee we also offer our heart-felt prayers, which we pour out in this place, with the conviction that they will ascend to Thy seat on high.

But, O Lord, mar not the hope which we are entitled to expect from Thy hands, and fulfil Thy promise לשמוע אל הרנה ואל התפלה graciously to accept every prayer of Thy subjects. Bestow Thy bounty on the poor one who comes to pray before Thee. Raise his despairing soul and inspire him with hope. Wipe, we beseech Thee, the hot tears of the widow, and solace the sorrowful heart of the orphan who comes to supplicate before Thee. Illumine their cabins and houses, and let them be convinced that Thy mercy *was*, *is*, and *will be* the Judge of the widow, and Father of the orphan.

From our innermost hearts we also pray, O Lord, for the peace and happiness of our gracious and beloved sovereign lady, Queen Victoria. Bless her with the love of the nations; with peace in her dominions, and with happiness in her family; and may she long continue to reign on the throne of her ancestors. Grant, also, O Lord, that our much beloved Albert Edward, Prince of Wales, may grow in glory like the strong cedar of Lebanon, and let his name shine like a star on the horizon. Guide and protect also, our estimable and trustworthy Governor, and all the Ministers and Servants of the Crown who mete out justice and spread truth, who propagate knowledge, who guard the peace, and devote their energies to their country's welfare. Bless also, O Lord, our congregation; the much-esteemed and trusted board of management, who have made great sacrifices for the accomplishment of this work. May peace and concord always prevail amongst them so that they work in unison, and call into existence many humane and charitable works.

Thus, my dear friends, I behold this sacred temple finished, founded by good men of whom Judaism may justly be proud. And to show that you acknowledge and appreciate the deeds of these good and noble men, it becomes you to share with them their due on this occasion, and give כף אחת עשרה וחב מלאה קטורת A handful of pure gold mixed with the incense of gratitude.

Hoping their honored names will be engraved on the hearts of the pious members of this congregation, who will venerate their memory which deserves everlasting recognition and whose feelings I at present endeavor to express.

The following criticisms on Dr. Jacobson's sermon appeared in the papers of the following day :—

" The rev. gentleman preached in English, and considering that three months since he could scarcely express himself in that language, his sermon was an eloquent one."—*Argus*.

" The Rev. Dr. Jacobson delivered an impassioned address. And as Dr. Jacobson has only been in the colony three or four months, and at the time he landed could not speak English, great astonishment was expressed at his eloquent discourse."—*Age*.

" And what was really the most interesting event of the ceremony took place. Dr. Düttner Jacobson, who has only been three months in the colony, and who when he came could neither understand nor speak the simplest sentence in English, was to preach for the first time in the language. Dr. Jacobson brought with him a reputation as an eminent Hebrew and Latin scholar. His preaching while here has been in German, and good German scholars who have heard him have spoken enthusiastically of his eloquence. That he should in three months be able to master English sufficiently to enable him to stand before a critical audience and preach an extempore sermon, was regarded as very hazardous. The rev. gentleman, however, more than justified his determination, and afforded ample proof that his repute for erudition and intellectual power was in no way exaggerated. His language was not only correct, but it was graceful, nervous and forcible ; and though much practice will be required before his pronunciation is free from peculiarity, it is even now quite inoffensive, and every word can be understood. The feat, as a linguistic and mental effort has probably never been surpassed."
—*Daily Telegraph*.

SERMON DELIVERED BY DR. JACOBSON, ON THE FIRST DAY ROSH HASHANA.

DEAR FRIENDS,—

We are told that when Moses had finished the writing of the Law, he commanded the bearers of the Ark לקח ארז ספר התורה הזאת to take this book of the Law ושמתם אותה מצד ארון ברית ד' place it beside the Ark of the Lord והיה שם בך לעד and shall there be as a witness against you. Indeed, the whole of our life is very much like a book! Our years and days form its divisions and chapters; and our deeds and works are the words and sentences which are noted in it. Three books, says the Talmud, are opened in Heaven on ר"ה day. In one of them, the sentence of the righteous is at once, without any delay, written down for everlasting life. In the second, the sentence of the irreclaimable sinner is immediately noted down to everlasting perdition. And the third book is open for the undecided, who are wavering in their minds, and whose sentence is reserved by the Heavenly Judge. To give a more lucid explanation, we shall see that this dictum of the Talmud means that the life of man appears before the Judge of the Universe in three different categories, namely— the pious, who fill up the days of their lives with works of truth and deeds of charity; those righteous people adorn and embellish with their own hands their records, so that their whole existence in this world becomes a ספר החיים a book of life, in which their names appear illuminated with honor and glory. On the other hand, the wicked and sinful, whose doings are ungodly, disfigure their book with images of death and corruption. Not a single ray of worth lights it up; not a single redeeming quality to plead for them—nothing but dark fiendish apparitions dwell in it, that at once drag them down into the bottomless pit. Again, those who are undecided and weakminded, who are continually wavering, vacillating and oscillating between Heaven and earth; the פוסחים על שתי סעיפים those who waver between two opinions, who jump from one thing to the other—now fearing God, and soon again committing sin; who are ready to change sides at any moment—such scrawl and illegible writing with which they fill their book of life the all-knowing God alone can read and understand.

Yes, dear friends, man is a blank, and his deeds and actions are accurately expressed on it in his own style, and as long that he takes care to preserve the balance between the corporeal and spiritual—that his imperishable and immortal soul receives as much aliment as his short-lived and corruptible body requires—he still may call himself master over his passions, and may confidently appear every morning before his Creator, and say אלהי נשמה שנתרת בי טהורה היא The soul which Thou hast entrusted to me is uncorrupted and preserved in her pristine purity without a blemish. Very different, however, is it with the negligent, who does not calculate, and is carried away by the stream of his natural desires and passions, wallowing in the mire of his sensuality. Such a man does not know what real pleasure is. He is unable to appreciate the bliss and happiness of him who calmly enjoys the pleasures of an undisturbed soul—of him who does not allow himself to be enslaved by his unlawful passions. Such a person's soul is continually bemoaning herself and complaining. She thus reasons with herself: "How deplorable my lot is to inhabit such a body! Tell me, all ye sluggish members, where is your solemn promise you made in the first hour of our meeting? Where is your tribute which you owe me? Where is your submission due to the heaven-born daughter which took up her temporary abode within you? Do you not know that I am mistress of the bodily abode? Are you not aware that your existence was solely created for my convenience? Do you forget that your proud dwelling-place will again become dark and desolate as soon that I leave it? Notwithstanding all that, I do not assume any authority over you; and all that I claim is the right of an undisturbed existence, without trying to encroach on your liberty. But you, members of the body, mock and scorn me! Not only do you snatch away from my mouth my scanty spiritual nourishment, but you even make me the tool of your base and hateful pursuits, and daily and hourly you plague me for your convenience, just like an impudent maid-servant who drives away her mistress." אדם יסודו כעפר Man's earthly garb, what more is it than a foreign substance? and after it has done its work, and no more of any use, is thrown away. And yet בנפשו יבא לחמו this foreign substance forces the rightful mistress to waive her privileges; to lower her position and provide man's requirements. In such a case, of course, the beautiful mechanism—man—becomes degraded. Because משל כחרס הנשבר כחצר יבש וכציץ נובל it debases his humanity, and degrades his destiny; his whole being is shattered and resembles a broken earthen vessel, mowed grass, and the faded flower: he, like those things, is in such a case disfigured and worthless.

Now, dear friends, let us read a passage from Holy Writ which bears on the subject, and faithfully illustrates our previous meditation. Right in the middle of the ninety-nine maledictions we find the following verse:— וכרתי את בריתי יצחק "And I will remember my covenant with Isaac, says the Lord, ואף את ברית אברהם אזכר I will also remember my covenant with

Abraham. וְהָאָרֶץ אֶזְכֹּר I shall also remember the Land." It is strikingly conspicuous that this piece of soothing consolation should have been inserted right in the midst of the most frightful maledictions, which make one's hair stand on end when reading them. However, according to our interpretation, that passage contains very little consolation indeed. In fact, it partakes more of the nature of a warning to the Israelitish nation than anything else. It is indisputable that Israel, if ever so fallen and deeply immersed in sin, can still hold its own, and favorably compare itself with the heathen nations. But the Lord says to them לְכוּ נָא וְנִוָּכְחָה Come, Israel, let us have our cause tried before another court. I am no more in a position to deliver judgment in a suit concerning myself. What is your plea? You always compare yourself with other nations, and show how much better you are than they. לְכוּ נָא אֵצֶל אֲבוֹתֵיכֶם If you are making comparisons, just compare yourself to the greatness and goodness of your own ancestors. And how would you then appear? A small figure, indeed, you would make alongside those giants of righteousness and piety. As to the comparison of Israel with the other nations of the world, we think that the case is similar to that of two criminals who were tried in a certain country for high treason. Both men were accused of one and the same crime, and both had an equal share in it. The judge inquired after their names, their antecedents, and their family connections. One told his interlocutor who he was, and who his relations were. But as soon as the judge heard who the prisoner's father was, he interrupted him, and told him he knew enough already. "Oh, so and so was your father! I have had the pleasure of making that gentleman's acquaintance many years ago; he was tried before me for murder, and was convicted. You belong to a very nice family! I have studied your pedigree. You belong to a brood of thieves and murderers; there is not a good one in the whole of your family." And now came the turn of the second prisoner to be examined. Him, also, the judge asked the same questions as he did of the first, to which the second prisoner very briefly replied, saying that his father was the celebrated preacher in such-and-such a place; his death was universally regretted and deeply lamented. And who was your father's father, again asked the judge? To which the prisoner answered that he also had been a great Rabbi in a certain province, where his memory is still venerated. Without hesitation, the judge sentenced him to longer imprisonment and to a severer punishment than his fellow-prisoner. This severe sentence was an unexpected thunderbolt which almost confounded him, and anxiously he asked the judge why his punishment should be severer than that of his accomplice, since they had both an equal share in the crime? Whereupon the judge explained to him, and gave him his reason. "You know," he said to the prisoner, "that the apple, as a rule, does not fall far from the tree. Your accomplice, of course, I know, was not less concerned in the committing of the crime than you. But you must not forget that he is a professional criminal and so were all his relations for many generations back. But with you the case is quite different. You belong to a noble race. You were brought up on the knees of a renowned and religious father, whose lineage is one of the noblest in the land. And now, tell me yourself if you don't deserve a greater punishment than the other prisoner, your accomplice? Remember you have disgraced your father in his grave! You have trampled with your own feet your noble pedigree!" The analogy between Israel and these two criminals is now self-evident.

By rights, Israel ought not to receive from God a severer punishment than the rest of the nations of the world, for the crimes of all of them are alike. But the question is here only of family connection and lineage. How; are the heathen nations also of noble origin? Canaan, from Ham; Javan, from Nimrod; Mizraim, from Ishmael; Edom, from Esau—a brood of criminals, of thieves and murderers, whose memory cannot be outraged.

Israel, on the other hand, can point to his ancestors with pride. And for this very reason, because they are proud of their ancestors, the degradation of their pride goes against them, and their sins weigh heavier in the scale of judgment. And, now we shall understand why that seemingly consoling verse appears amongst the most frightful maledictions. והאבתי אותם בארץ אויביהם The Thora forewarns Israel "I shall let you be carried away into the land of your enemies ואו ירצו את עונם to give me satisfaction for your sins" But do you know the reason why I shall deal so mercilessly with you, because וזכרתי את בריתי יעקב *because* I will bear in mind that I made a covenant with Jacob; on whose knees you were nursed and brought up, I cannot forget. ואף את בריתי יצחק ואף את בריתי אברהם אזכר And because I also shall remember who your grandfather and your great-grandfather were; therefore, והארץ תעזב מהם therefore you must leave the country—a punishment which I would not inflict on other nations. In the same manner, and for the same reason, does the Israelitish nation as a whole, and every individual Israelite for himself, form an exception on ר"ה As often that the Jewish new year begins, so often again that day reminds us with its doleful and merry impressions, that everyone of us ought to examine himself again. We ought to examine again our book of life, and read it through carefully, so that the person may—though not knowing with certainty what is in store for him to happen during the next year—at least to be able to guess and imagine what might happen.

The unhappy one, dear friends, whose book of life till now was nothing but a מגלת איכה "a collection of woes and sorrows," wherein nothing but sighs and tears were inserted, and from beginning to end is almost filled with דברי צומות וזעקות hunger and lamentations. Let that unhappy one pay attention to the merry and joyous impressions of this ר' ה' day; and let him return to his God, who will take pity of him, and order his angels—כתבו על היהודים כטוב בעיניכם Write down in that godly man's book his own wishes and desires, and let his מגלת איכה be changed into a מגלת שה"ש into a book of joyful songs, in which henceforth may be read ששון ושמחה ישיגו ונסו יגון ואנחה Happiness and joy shall be his lot, sorrow and care far from his cot.

And the happy one—he who is already in possession of such a book—let him mark and pay attention to the doleful impressions of the ר' ה' day, and let him endeavor to devote himself the more to that which is good and noble, so that he may remain blessed, and that the blessings which he enjoys at present might not be changed into curses. Let him take care that his soul should not self-guiltily accuse herself before God. ואם אין מחני נא מספרך אשר כתבת Forgive me, O Lord, my transgressions; and if not, blot out my name from Thy book, which Thou hast written; and that the Lord should not have to reply מי אשר חטא לי אמחנו מספרי Yes, he who sins before me, I will blot out from my book. And let the miser and avaricious, who till now has only followed the call of his passions, which urged him to take a great tablet and write on it in large characters למהר שלל חש בז " Plunder and rob quickly." Let him on this ר'ה' day crush " this great tablet" under the mountain of his stony heart, and let him acquire in its place the tablets of Israel's covenant. He who is friendless and quarrelsome, whose book of life is a כ' מלחמות a book of wars which he constantly carries about him, and is even at war with himself; and את והב בסופה is continually foaming and dashing his violent waves: him let the ר'ה' day remind עוכר שארו אכזרי that he is his own cruel enemy. Him let God give quietness, and bless him with peace.

And the pious one, who has always been leading an enviable course of life: him let the ר' ה' day remind, and urge to new perseverance in doing good and noble deeds; and let him continue his ס' הישר; his book of righteousness; his ס' המצוות; his book of duties; his ס' התורה; his book of the Law: and, finally, his ס' החכמה his book of wisdom, in which his noble deeds may be inscribed and handed down to posterity, and which the Lord God looks upon with pleasure, and commands his servants כתוב זאת זכרון בספר The man's name who in my book is reported shall have no sorrow nor be heavy-hearted; but joy, love and happiness to him be allotted.

Dear friends, as I am not in the position to know your individual inclinations, wants, desires and wishes; and not being able to wish every one of you separately that your prayers may have been accepted; believe me, therefore, to have discharged a small part of my duty if I wish you all together from the depth of my heart a שנת ברכה ושלום a year full of blessings and happiness.

May God Almighty, in the year ה'ר' ל' ח' increase your wealth a thousandfold, and may you obtain all and everything according to your own wishes. אמן.

SERMON PREACHED BY DR. JACOBSON ON THE EVE OF THE DAY OF ATONEMENT.

שומר מה מלילה Watchman, what of the night? שומר מה מליל אמר שומר אתה בוקר וגם לילה Watchman, what from the night? The watchman says, "The morning comes after the night!" אם תבעיון בעיו שובו אתיו If you wish to ask more questions, come some other time.

The night of the tenth of *Tishri* has once more arrived;—it is the day on which Israel sheds oceans of tears! If you look round, you will see that whilst one is complaining of his hard and unbearable lot, another is sighing and lamenting over some fatal disease which gnaws at his vitals; and perhaps in the third corner a still more appalling sight will meet your eye. There, widows and orphans, deep in mourning, are weeping; shedding hot tears, bemoaning their desolate condition. Into that corner the bright sheen of our temple does not penetrate; and, notwithstanding the numerous burning lights, total darkness reigns in their hearts. There is no balm for their wounds, no consolation for the treasures which death has snatched away from them, and are now reposing in the silent grave. Too great is their affliction; and, therefore, the Almighty צבאות readily allows them to avail themselves of His mercies, held out to them on the tenth of *Tishri*. ומחר אעשה כדבר המלך Yes, and to-morrow is the day appointed on which the King's command will be executed.

The מסורה gives a different reading of the passage just quoted. It reads: ויחר אהרן ויש אחך "Do not say I shall give to-morrow when you can give to-day," says Solomon. And Samuel says— וכחר אתה ובניך עמי "To-morrow, King Saul, shalt thou and thy sons be with me." And, again, we find that the Lord ordered

Israel וְקִדַּשְׁתָּם הַיּוֹם וּמָחָר וְכִבְּסוּ שִׂמְלוֹתָם "Sanctify yourself to-day and to-morrow, and wash your garments." Oh, how difficult it is for me, dear friends, to make you understand the full meaning and the great import of the exhortations contained in those scattered passages. Let me, therefore, try with the aid of a simple illustration to explain them. A merchant who was about to go on a long journey assembled before his departure the whole of his family to wish them farewell. His children noticed in him an unusual sadness, and inquired for its cause. "You have left us many times before, dear father," the children said to him, "and you never were so sad as on this occasion." "Ah, dear children," answered he, " you wish to know the reason ? Know, then, that the road which I am to travel this time is a very dangerous one, and many are the accidents that have happened on it to other travellers. Suppose, now, that I assembled you an hour before my death, should I then not be sad? And this, also, might be our last meeting, for who can tell what will happen." And now, dear friends, you will understand what this illustration has to do with the subject of my discourse.

Two seasons are offered to Israel for repentance. The Day of Atonement is the season for the whole nation; and the last hour before parting from our earthly sojourn is the individual Israelite's time to repent. מִי שֶׁחָלָה וְנָטָה לָמוּת אוֹמְרִים לוֹ הִתְוַדֵּה " Whosoever is near his death," say our sages, "ask him to repent." In former days, when the world was several thousand years younger, it was quite different to what it is now. Then the human race was healthy, strong, and robust, and sickness was almost a thing unknown. In those days the יה"כ was not observed exclusively as a day of lamentation and repentance. In those days every person could safely rely on his calm conscience, and commence his journey without any misgivings, hoping that sufficient time would be left to him for repenting before his death. But very different it is at present. Now the human race is subject to all kinds of diseases. We are harassed by troubles and cares; obstacles are met with at each step and moment of our life. אֵין שָׁעָה בְּלֹא רָעָה וְאֵין רֶגַע בְּלֹא פֶּגַע Not an hour passes without affliction, and no moment without that some accident happens. No, in our days we cannot and dare not put off our confessions and repentance. If we think it well with ourselves, we must embrace the first opportunity which offers itself to us, and not wait lest it grow dark and it be too late. Just carry back your memory, dear friends, for a few moments, and think of those who have been with us last יה"כ, but are no more amongst us here to-night. Think of those who last יה"כ still prayed with you here. וְיֶהֱגֶה מִי לְכַם פֹּה Say do you not notice the considerable gap which has been left since ? Whom did the departed leave in their places? Whom did they leave? Inconsolable wives with broken hearts and unhappy children! And are we better off than those who passed away from amongst us? And that is what the מסורה says: Take care, son of Israel! Do not trust to the promptings of your wicked inclinations, saying there is yet time enough to repent; יבא היום אל המשחה in your excitement and freaks of folly, you think that being strong and healthy you may go on enjoying yourself, for you think that evil is yet far off, ומחר אעשה כדבר המלך and to-morrow will be time enough to give account of yourself to the King. But you must remember ומחר אהן ויש אתך I advise you not to put trust in the morrow, if you can do it to-day, whilst you are with me. For ומחר אהה ובניך עמי how do you know that to-morrow you shall not have already begun your journey, and departed from this world without having carried out your intentions ומחר אל כל עדת ישראל יקצוף and an innocent Israel shall have to suffer for your negligence in leaving unforgiven sins behind. And, therefore, וקדשתם היום ומחר וכבסו שמלותכם accomplish to-day what you intend to do to-morrow. Cleanse yourself of your iniquities עד אשר לא יבואו ימי הרעה before death has entered in your house. Do not be ashamed to confess before your God that which never was a secret to Him. Kneel down and be your own high priest in the sanctuary of sanctuaries, and say אנא השם עויתי Oh, Father, I have fatally wounded myself אנא השם כפר Oh, Father, come quickly to my rescue! Amen.

MICKVEH YISRAEL

East Melbourne Hebrew Congregation,

ESTABLISHED MARCH 5617–1857.

PRESIDENTS AND TREASURERS

OF THE

East Melbourne Hebrew Congregation

FROM ITS FOUNDATION.

Year.	President.	Treasurer.
1858-5619 ...	M. NELSON	S. SOLOMON
1859-5620 ...	M. NELSON	J. HART
1860-5621 ...	M. NELSON	*ABM. WOLFF
		L. DAVIS
1861-5622 ...	L. DAVIS	S. COHEN
1862-5623 ...	L. DAVIS	S. COHEN
1863-5624 ...	L. DAVIS	A. WAXMAN
1864-5625 ...	S. SOLOBERG	A. WAXMAN
1865-5625 ...	H. J HART	M. ANDERSON.
1866-5626 ...	H. I. HART	M. ANDERSON
1867-5627 ...	H. J. HART	L. C. GERSCHEL
1868-5629 ...	H. J. HART	L. C. GERSCHEL
1869-5629 ...	L. C. GERSCHEL	A. WAXMAN
1870-5630 ...	A. WAXMAN	W. DAVIS
1871-5631 ...	A. WAXMAN	W. DAVIS
1872-5632 ...	W. DAVIS	J. COHEN
1873-5633 ...	W. DAVIS	J. COHEN
1874-5634 ...	J. COHEN	‡L. C. GERSCHEL
1875-5635 ...	H. J HART	M. HERMAN
1876-5636 ...	H. J. HART	M. HERMAN
1877-5637 ...	A. WAXMAN	M. HERMAN

* *Resigned.* ‡ *Resigned.*

ESTABLISHMENT

OF THE

East Melbourne Hebrew Congregation

The most striking feature of the Jewish Synagogue is the singular unity of its history. Since the dispersion of the people and the close of their political existence, its annals know no schism of any kind. No new doctrines have risen to confound the intellect or disturb the faith of its professors. The Jewish creed, long ago rooted in the hearts of the children of Israel, is one and indivisible, and is beyond the power of false prophets, and no deceptive teachers can sever the ties that unite communities, or to effect that separation of congregations which is so unenviable a feature in younger religions.

Doubtless some straggler, like a withered leaf, may occasionally drop off from the tree of the nation. But the Jews in all parts of the world, bound together by many and peculiar ties, in spite of ages of envy, hate, and persecution, still preserve a firm and unbroken national existence. The teachings of the rabbis of to-day are identical with those of their predecessors ages ago, and neither the fires of Torquemado nor the sword of Mahomed has ever forced them to adopt any modification of that great law committed to them by Jehovah himself amidst the thunders of Sinai. Not one jot or tittle has been altered; and in the most distant regions of the earth the Jew still hears within the walls of his Synagogue the same familiar tongue and the same familiar and revered worship. Throughout the whole world the use of the Hebrew language confirms the unity of the Jewish faith.

However, as in old times, political and social causes have operated to produce temporary separation, so in modern days, whenever large bodies of Jews are associated, differences of opinion will sometimes arise, though in matters of management only; and this happened in Melbourne soon after Judaism had been established on a firm basis.

In the year 1857, the Rev. Moses Rintel, who was one of the pioneers of Judaism in the colony, and the first authorised Jewish minister, resigned his position at the West Melbourne Synagogue, which led to the establishing of another place of worship.

In March, 1857, a numerous meeting of the Jewish community residing in the east end of the city was held for the purpose of founding a local Synagogue, which was at once established under the name of the "Mikveh Yisrael Melbourne Synagogue." Mr. Solomon Solomon was elected president, and the late Mr. M. Nelson treasurer. The Rev. M. Rintel consenting to officiate as minister, they at once proceeded to and obtained the necessary registration, and secured their right to the use of the burial-ground and mortuary chapel. The first service was held in Spring-street (in the premises formerly used as the Melbourne Grammar School), and in consequence of the increase of its members, more extensive premises were leased in Great Lonsdale-street east.

Through the exertions of the Rev. M. Rintel, Messrs. Nelson, Henri J. Hart, and Moritz Michaelis, the congregation obtained a grant of land in Stephen-street, and the foundation-stone was laid on Wednesday, the 28th December, 5620—1859, by Mr. Nelson, the president for that year.

The form of service on the occasion was as follows :—The congregation assembled in the building occupied by them as a temporary synagogue, situated in Lonsdale-street east, at four o'clock p.m., where, after Mincha (afternoon service), the following Psalms were read in alternate verses by the minister and congregation—viz., 24th, 29th, 30th, 93rd, 100th, 122nd, and 132nd. The ark was then opened, and all the congregation rising, the usual prayer for the Queen and Royal Family was read. The Rev. M. Rintel delivered an address, taking for his text the 1st, 2nd, 4th and 5th verses of the 35th chapter of Numbers. He remarked that as all the necessary works for the erection of the tabernacle had to be done by Jewish hands, Moses feared they would in their zeal for its completion violate the Sabbath-day. Moses, therefore, wisely and timely cautioned them against the commission of so great a sin. He also quoted from several commentaries, to show that they were actuated in a great desire to appease the wrath of God and propitiate for the sin of making and worshipping the golden calf. He alluded to the manner in which they responded to the call, and pointed out the fact that the Almighty was as much pleased with the small amounts offered by the poor man as the larger offerings made by the wealthy ; as observed by the Talmud—"It is one (to the Almighty) whether it be a large or a small offering, so long as it is accompanied with the heart." But (observed the rev. lecturer), independently of subscribing our share when required for any good purpose, we have other important duties to perform. As parents, we are bound to provide proper education for our children. He then briefly traced the position of the Jews in Great Britain from an early period, when nought but oppression and persecutions were their share. He contrasted their present state to that of days long gone by, and especially their standing as colonists here. All denominations being placed upon an equal footing, Jews here could hold the highest offices in the State, which rendered it the more desirable that they should be properly educated. Nor should their duty to God be neglected. It behoved parents to accustom their children at a very early and tender age to repeat short and appropriate prayers, which tended to instil into their minds the fear of the Lord. After pointing out the great advantages to be gained by proper knowledge and learning, he concluded with the following prayer:—

"And we supplicate Thee, O Universal Lord! at whose command all things were called into existence, and from whom all living creatures derive their being, in thine infinite kindness and love didst Thou select us from all other nations, and hast sanctified us with Thy commands. But, O Lord, through our iniquities and sins were we cast out of our holy land, and scattered away among all nations. In the land of our enemies have we suffered from the sword, starvation, burning, drawing, and innumerable other sufferings, yet didst Thou not entirely forsake us, nor give us up to destruction.

"In all our agonies we acknowledged Thy unity, and founded our reliance upon Thee as the rock of our salvation.

"We now enjoy greater freedom, and under the shelter of our Most Gracious Sovereign Lady Queen Victoria, we are in full possession of protection and freedom.

"Grant, we beseech Thee, O Lord, unto her and her subjects the fulness of Thy blessing; as, also, bless our beloved Ruler and Governor, Sir Henry Barkly. Crown him with health and happiness. Vouchsafe to prosper the undertaking, which is intended both as a house of prayer and a school, wherein Thy holy laws and sacred knowledge may be imparted to the rising generation of the Hebrew faith. May this new edifice, of which the cornerstone is this day to be laid, be founded on stability; may the light and truth rest thereon, so that Thy nation may be endowed with the spirit of prudence and wisdom, the spirit of counsel and light, the spirit of knowledge and fear of the Lord! Amen.

The offerings towards the new building were then announced, and upwards of £300 subscribed. The procession was then formed, M. Krohn, Esq., acting as M.C., in the following order, viz.:—

Messrs. Knight and Kerr, architects.
Mr. George Connon, builder.
The Rev. Moses Rintel, minister of the congregation.
Supported by M. Nelson, Esq., President; and A. Wolff, Esq., Treasurer.

Followed by the Trustees, the Committee, and the members of the community, walking four abreast.

On the arrival at the ground, Mr. B. Rapiport presented, in a neat speech, a silver trowel to M. Nelson, Esq., bearing a suitable inscription. The Hebrew portion of the scroll was read by the minister, and the English by Mr. M. Capua, as follows:—

"With the assistance of Almighty God,
"To commemorate the laying of the foundation-stone of the Jewish School, in connection with the Mickveh Yisrael, East Melbourne Synagogue, on the 28th day of December, 1859—5620, by M. Nelson, Esq., President, assisted by the Rev. M. Rintel, minister, and Abm. Wolff, Treasurer, in the 23rd year

of the reign of Her Majesty Queen Victoria, Sir Henry Barkly, Governor of the Colony. Members of Committee—Messrs. J. Bloomington, L. Davis, E. Rich, A. Waxman, B. Rapaport, S. Soleberg, M. Capua, hon. sec.; M. Goldstein and Joseph Avinski, trustees; Rev. M. Rintel, Henri J. Hart, J.P., M. Michaelis, M. Nelson, and Abraham Wolff, Esqs.; Mr. Samuel Saunders, collector; and Mr. J. M. Goldreich, shochet."

The President then spread the mortar, and the scroll, in a hermetically sealed jar, having been deposited in the cavity of the stone, the minister offered the following prayers, first in Hebrew and then in English, viz. :—

"May it be Thy will, O Lord, Creator of Heaven and Earth, to enable the building of this house to be carried on successfully to its completion. May Thy blessing overtake the work thus begun, and Thy holy name be established therein."

The President having applied the square level and plumb-rule, the ceremony of using wine, corn, and oil, was proceeded with, and the minister offered the second prayer, viz. :—

"May the bountiful hand of Heaven ever supply this province with abundance of corn, wine, and oil, and all necessaries of life. May He whose mighty hand encompasseth eternity be the Guard and Protector over this city and its inhabitants, and may He long preserve this building from peril and decay. Amen."

The President then gave three knocks with the mallet, and declared the stone justly laid. He then spoke as follows :—

"My Friends,—It is not my intention to trouble you with a lengthened address, since I know full well that I neither possess the talent nor ability required for so difficult a task. But I feel that I should be unworthy of the honor conferred upon me were I entirely to abstain from expressing my sentiments in reference to the important ceremony of the day. When we seriously reflect on the wonderful formation of the world, how soon our mind becomes lost in the vast abyss of Creation! Wherever we look, on whatever we gaze, His marvellous acts declare His wisdom and power. Not only is He the author of our being, but also the creator of all that we see around us. He has endued man with a Divine competency, in order that He might prosecute His researches into the innermost secrets of nature, and thereby further develop the numerous hidden treasures of arts and sciences which surround him on all sides. This knowledge is acquired by means of study conveyed to the mind by a proper system of education. It is to be hoped, my friends, that you will not consider your attendance here this day to assist me in laying the first foundation-stone sufficient, but that you will continue to afford us your assistance and support in carrying out the several objects for which this edifice is intended—objects both sacred and important. May the all-wise Providence who in His goodness and mercy has allowed us to lay the foundation-stone this day, preserve and protect the building from decay, and grant that the institution may flourish and thrive. (Cheers.) May we be prosperous and successful in all our undertakings, that we may perfect what we have begun. May our offspring, for many succeeding years, assemble within its walls to receive the light of knowledge and understanding, and may our orisons offered therein ascend to "Heaven, His dwelling-place." For such sacred and noble purposes is the structure which we are about to raise intended, the foundation-stone of which you have permitted me to lay. In conclusion, my friends, accept my most sincere, cordial, and heartfelt thanks for the mark of respect and privilege you have bestowed on me, in allowing me to afford my humble assistance in so meritorious and holy a work."

A small building was erected, which was opened for divine worship in 1860. For a long time Mr. Rintel officiated without receiving any remuneration for his arduous and self-imposed duties. And not until the services attracted a large number of wealthy and influential citizens did the officiating ministers receive salaries.

When, however, it was found that the situation of the Synagogue was objectionable, on account of the locality, and that the number of worshippers was too great for the building, efforts were made to bring about an amalgamation of the two metropolitan congregations, with a view to the erection of a large and central place of worship. For some reasons, however, these efforts were unsuccessful, and the Mikveh Yisrael congregation decided on building for themselves a new Synagogue, and was brought to a successful issue, principally through the exertions of

THE TRUSTEES, Viz.:—

Rev. Moses Rintel   Henri J. Hart, Esq., J.P.
Aaron Waxman, Esq.   Marks Herman, Esq.
Joseph Cohen, Esq.   Edward Rich, Esq.
Emanuel Steinfeld, Esq. J.P. Samuel De Beer., Esq.
Joseph Levy, Esq.

And the Executive of the Synagogue for the present year :—

President:
HENRI J. HART, Esq., J.P.

Treasurer:
MARKS HERMAN, Esq.

Committee:

Aaron Waxman, Esq.   Joseph Cohen, Esq.
Edward Rich, Esq.   Samuel De Beer, Esq.
Philip Perlstein, Esq.   Abraham Loel, Esq.
Mark Marks, Esq.   Leopold Kraetzer, Esq.

A site was purchased at a cost of £2500, opposite the Parliamentary Reserve, and the foundation-stone was laid on Tuesday, 20th March, 1877.

The ceremony of laying the memorial stone was preceded by a special service, held at three o'clock, in the Synagogue in Stephen street, which was conducted by the Revs. E. Blaubaum, J. M. Goldreich, R. Benjamin, S. Greenbaum, and other ministers. The ministers, trustees of the Synagogue, and the office-bearers, accompanied by a number of the leading members of the congretion, then proceeded to the site of the new Synagogue (adjoining the Albert-street Baptist Church), where the preparations had been completed for the laying of the stone. The proceedings commenced by the reading of an address by the Rev. Moses Rintel, who said the occasion which had caused them to assemble was one of no ordinary character. It was an evidence of the increase of the believers of the venerable faith of Israel in this influential city, and also to a certain extent a proof of the general prosperity of the community of which they formed an integral part. He referred to the principal motives which actuated the congregation in determining to erect a new place of worship. They wished in the first place to give the Eternal a small proof of their gratitude towards him for his many favors towards them : they desired, secondly, to have a becoming edifice in which they and their wives and children might meet together to perform the sacred ordinances of their holy faith ; and, lastly, by no means an objectionable motive, especially by the erection of a synagogue in close proximity to various other places of worship, they wished to show their fellow-citizens that although there might be some external differences in the formularies of the various religious beliefs, yet the intention of all was the same. They would be taught that God was the Father of us all, and that we were therefore all brethren, and were bound as such to help each other in every possible way, and instead of endeavoring to add fuel to the flames of ancient feuds and quarrels, to consider how we might turn the cursed fire of discord into the life-giving warmth of friendship ; for those doctrines alone were worthy of the name of religion which tended to unite men together in the love of each other and of their God. The great object we should all propose to ourselves in our various congregations was that next to the paramount duty of loving God, our most important work was to love each other, and to help each other in distress and trouble, irrespective of country or creed. The building which was about to be raised would also be used as a school for the instruction of their children, and as all learning, when properly used, led us nearer to the Eternal, even this intended use of the building should stimulate them to be as zealous as possible in bringing it to a speedy conclusion. In conclusion, he urged the necessity of their contributing to the building fund as much as possible, imitating the alacrity with which their forefathers had responded to the invitation of the great King to contribute to the service of the House of God.

On the conclusion of the address, prayer was offered in Hebrew and English by the Rev. Mr. Goldreich, after which the treasurer, Mr. Herman, by direction of the committee, presented to the president a handsome silver trowel with which to perform the ceremony. The trowel bore the inscription :—

EAST MELBOURNE HEBREW CONGREGATION.

PRESENTED TO HENRI J. HART, ESQ., J.P., PRESIDENT, ON THE OCCASION OF LAYING THE FOUNDATION STONE OF THE NEW SYNAGOGUE IN ALBERT STREET. 20TH MARCH, 5637—1877.

Mr. Hart returned his sincere thanks for the gift, which he said he would always keep as a memorial of this very important occasion.

Several psalms were then sung, and the Rev. Mr. Rintel read the scroll containing the date of the ceremony and the names of officers of the synagogue, the architects, and contractors. The scroll, with the newspapers of the day, were then deposited by the president in the stone, after which prayer was again offered by the Rev. E. Blaubaum. The stone was then lowered, and laid by the president in the customary manner, pouring over it corn, wine, and oil. The Rev. R. Benjamin then in Hebrew and English invoked the following blessing on the work:—"May the bountiful hand of Heaven ever supply this province with abundance of corn, wine, and oil, and all the necessaries of life. May He whose mighty hand encompasseth Eternity be the guard and protector over this young city and its inhabitants, and may He long preserve this building from peril and decay. Amen."

The President, Mr. H. J. Hart, then delivered a brief address. He said this congregation had now been established 20 years, and was an offshoot from the older congregation in Bourke-street. The congregation had to contend with a great many difficulties, but they had been all overcome, and he hoped that a bright future was in store which will be satisfactory to all the members of the congregation. The career of this congregation probably might find a parallel in the career of the Jews in ancient times. At the destruction of the Temple the Jews were dispersed, and were to be found in the remotest corners of the world. Traces of their residence were found in Northern Asia, in Africa, in North and South America, but the larger bulk of them found homes on the Continent of Europe. At the destruction of the first Temple, it is related in history that they first found a home in Alexandria, in Egypt, and at one time there were upwards of 100,000 Jews resident in that great city. Persecutions, however, scattered them to Europe, where they suffered many persecutions: Within the last 100 years, or perhaps more properly 50 years, however, the Jews as a body had attained a position of which they may be proud. (Applause.) In happy England they had, by perseverance, broken down all the barriers which prevented them from rising to political or social eminence, until Jews were now found in the most leading positions in Great Britain. He referred also to the eminence attained by men of the Jewish religion in the United States. He referred to Judge Noah, Judge Joachim, Admiral Levy, and other men of note. In New South Wales, Mr. Saul Samuel had held the post of Treasurer, and had been decorated by her Majesty with the order of St. Michael and St. George, and Mr. Julian Salamans, the eminent barrister, held the position of Solicitor-General; while, belonging to New Zealand, there was Sir Julius Vogel; and in Victoria there was the hon.

Edward Cohen, who had filled the honorable position of Commissioner of Customs, and had always taken an active part in every matter appertaining to religion, education, or social progress. (Applause.) In conclusion, he expressed a hope that before six months were over the present building would be opened, and he besought their steady help and encouragement to enable it to be made worthy of its objects.

Psalm lxvii. was then sung, and the ceremony terminated with cheers for the Queen, the Governor, the mayor of Melbourne, and the ladies.

Description of the Synagogue.

The Synagogue has a frontage of 42ft. to Albert-street, a depth of 73ft., and a height of 31ft. The main entrance is approached by a flight of steps, and the central door opens into a hall, upon each side of which stand cloak rooms. Through these rooms the congregation can pass either to the floor of the Synagogue or to the balcony, which is reached by a pair of staircases. Accommodation is provided for about 470 worshippers. The furniture at present in use is from the Stephen-street Synagogue. At the north end of the room are conspicuous marble steps, which lead up to the היכל. Over the entrance to the היכל are written in Hebrew the Ten Commandments. On each side of the table are tablets on which will be inscribed, in English and in Hebrew, the prayer offered for the Queen and the Royal Family. Within and without, the Synagogue is a handsome, well-constructed edifice. Mr. Tobin's plan of ventilation has been adopted to keep the atmosphere of the interior always pure. The cost of the Synagogue, exclusive of that of the land, is £7,000. At the rear stands a schoolroom, which for the present will be used for the religious instruction of the young. The hall is illuminated by two sunlights, and a pair of candelabra 8ft. high, erected in front of the entrance to the tabernacle.

The Consecration.

The formal opening of the Synagogue took place on Wednesday evening, the 27th Ellul, 5637 (5th September, 1877). In addition to the members of the congregation, there were many of the leading Jewish citizens present, and many Christian residents of Melbourne. At eight o'clock the doors were closed, and the voices of the choir were heard outside the building—

שאו שערים ראשיכם והנשאו פתחי עולם ויבא מלך הכבוד

In response to a knock, accompanied by the chanting of—

פתחו לי שערי צדק אבא בכ אודה יה

the doors were opened, and the Revs. Samuel Herman, Dr. Dättner Jacobson, Raphael Benjamin, Elias Blaubaum, S. Greenbaum, and Mr. Henri J. Hart, entered, carrying the scrolls of the law, the latter handing over his scroll to the Rev. Moses Rintel. The ministers named, then made the seven circuits round the Synagogue, reciting portions of Psalms xxx., xlii., Ibid, v. 7, xliii., cxxx., c., and the xxix. by the choir. All the scrolls but one were then placed in the ark, and the Rev. Moses Rintel gave a prayer for the Royal Family, after which the rev. gentleman delivered a sermon.

The service terminated with an offertory, which was well responded to. The choir, which was conducted by Mr. Louis Pulver, sang very nicely during the ceremony, and did great credit to that young gentleman's musical attainments.

THE REV. MOSES RINTEL

was born in the year 1823, in Edinburgh, Scotland, and was educated for the ministry in London, under Dr. Sulzberger. In 1844 he arrived in Sydney, where he was engaged in teaching Hebrew until 1849, the year in which he removed to Melbourne, and was appointed minister of the Melbourne Hebrew Congregation, with the understanding that the Rev. Dr. Adler, the Chief Rabbi in London, confirm the appointment. Since 1849 he has watched the progress of Judaism in the colony. The rev. gentleman has recently recovered from a very severe illness; but it is hoped by all who know him that his assumption of duties in the new building is but the prelude to a renewed and prolonged career of usefulness.

MR. HENRI J. HART.

With reference to that gentleman, we feel it our duty to say a few words. Mr. Hart has identified himself with the interests of Judaism in Melbourne from its earliest days. He was honorary secretary to the youthful congregation for three years, and his services were acknowledged by the congregation, on his retirement from the office, by presenting him on the New Year 5611— 1850 with a handsome testimonial "for the zealous and efficient manner in which he discharged the multifarious duties of that office." Since 1857, the year in which Mr. Rintel severed his connection with the Melbourne Hebrew Congregation, Mr. Hart was a warm supporter in every enterprise calculated to advance the interest of the East Melbourne Hebrew Congregation. In 1870 the members of the congregation presented him with a magnificent service of plate, consisting of a centre epergne and two side pieces to match, in recognition of his valuable services as President during a period of four years. The gift was accompanied with an address on parchment setting forth the resolutions of the annual general meeting to acknowledge his services in a suitable manner.

SERMON DELIVERED BY THE REV. MOSES RINTEL, ON THE OCCASION OF THE OPENING OF THE NEW ALBERT STREET SYNAGOGUE, EAST MELBOURNE.

(Verbatim Report.)

ה' אהבתי מעון ביתך ומקום משכן כבודך

O Lord! I have loved the habitation of Thy house and the dwelling-place of Thy glory. (Ps. xxvi. 8.)

My dear brethren,—Words cannot express the feeling of my heart this day. Deeply and sincerely grateful do I feel unto the Most High, that He הגומל לחייבים טובות did not suffer the torrent of sickness to overwhelm me, but brought me through my affliction, and allowed me to gain strength sufficient to be with you on this day, so full of joy to each one of us. Verily he is אל עושה פלא a God of wonders, and His greatness is above all His works. Blessed for ever be His holy name! and may all heaven and earth unite with us in chanting His praises: יהללוהו שמים וארץ ימים וכל רמש בם " Let the heaven and earth praise Him, the seas, and everything that moveth therein"—(Ps. lxix. 34); and let the burden of our united song be expressed in these beautiful words— ה' אהבתי מעון ביתך ומקום משכן כבודך "Oh, Lord! I have loved the habitations of Thy house and the dwelling-place of Thy glory.'

If every pulsation of our heart were an offering of love to the Most High, and if every farthing of our worldly possessions were to be devoted to His service, we know that we should but be offering to Him what is already His own. The Eternal cannot be enriched by our poor offerings, nor could the canticles of the whole world add the slightest increase to His glory. But he has said ויקחו לי תרומה ועשו לי וכו' out of regard for the creatures of His love. He is pleased to accept our poor offerings, as though they were really ours to give, and as though He were honored and enriched by the gifts of our hands.

Let us be assured then, dear brethren, that He will look with complacency down from His throne, amid the cherubim and seraphim, when we this day make a solemn offering to Him for this בית מקדש מעט minor temple which you in your devotion and piety have built for the celebration of the services of our holy faith and for the honor and worship of His adorable Majesty.

We know that מלא כל הארץ כבודו "His immensity filleth all space," both actual and possible, and that the gloomiest recesses in the darkest and deepest caves are lit up with His light. ה' אמר לשכן בערפל (מלכים א'ח' כ"ב) " The Lord hath said that He will dwell in darkness." But it is not in the midst of darkness that He invites His faithful children to come and worship Him on his sabbaths and festivals. No, He puts it into the hands of His children to build beautiful temples to Him—buildings which by their splendor may allure our little ones to His service, and induce them to love the habitation of His house and the dwelling-place of His glory, and make them think of the ineffable beauty of that great Temple above, in which the Eternal will reward all those who while on earth have been faithful to the observance of His holy precepts.

It is not the Lord who stands in need of temples, for the whole universe is to Him a temple; but we, His creatures, require these buildings that are specially dedicated to Him to remind us that while we are in them we must not allow our minds to be filled with our everyday thoughts— thoughts of power and wealth —of speculations, and business, and all such worldly things—but to fix them on the things of eternity, and try to fit ourselves for the duties of Heaven by praising the Eternal, and like the wisest of all kings acknowledge—ה׳ אלהי ישראל אין כמוך אלהים בשמים ובארץ שמר הברית והחסד לעבדיך ההלכים לפניך בכל לבם (ר׳ה׳י ו׳ י׳ד) "O Lord God of Israel, there is none like Thee in the heavens nor in the earth; which keepest the covenant and showest mercy unto Thy servants that walk before Thee with all their hearts." (2 Ch., vi. 14.)

True it is that even in our own *homes*, we are bound by the laws of our holy faith to think often of our God, and to let the aspirations of our hearts float upwards to His throne, begging for that divine assistance which is constantly needed by those who wish to lead a pure and holy life. But—speaking more worldly— even as the votaries of pleasure, not satisfied with what they can find in their own abodes, build theatres and halls to give them extra enjoyments, so we build *temples* to our God, that in them our hearts may be inebriated with the fulness of joy that is vouchsafed to those who make it their delight to walk in the way of His commandments.

How many and how beautiful are the lessons that will be taught us and our children in this holy place! Hither the poor wayfarer will come and take his place under the same roof with the wealthiest of the land, and may feel that he is the child of the same God who caused the son of David to build a glorious temple to His name, and as he (immediately on entering) beholds the sacred Ten Commandments, and as he looks towards the holy spot wherein are enshrined the ספרי תורות scrolls of the Law, he will not fail to exclaim ה׳ אהבת מעון ביתך ומקום משכן כבודך "O Lord, I have loved the habitation of Thy house and the dwelling-place of Thy glory."

Yes, my dear brethren, you who have cheerfully devoted a portion of your worldly means for building this sacred edifice to the honor and glory of the Eternal, and a school for the religious instruction of our children, may assuredly speak words of comfort unto your souls this day. You may thank the Eternal for having enabled you to take a part in such noble works. You may feel that you have not been forgetful of your obligations to honor Him with your substance, and to prove to the children of other faiths that the sons and daughters of Israel are still sensible of all that their God did for them in times past; and that in these days when the truths of eternity are little thought of by men, or are submitted to the chilling influence of rationalism, we are still anxious to avail ourselves of all external means of fostering a lively recollection of the great deeds of the mighty past, and of the mysterious covenant that has subsisted, and is to subsist for all ages, between the Eternal and us the children of Israel.

In a spirit of humble confidence that our prayer will be answered, we may therefore address the Eternal this day, saying, ופנית אל תפלת עבדך ואל תחנתו ה' אלהי לשמע אל הרנה ואל התפלה אשר עבדך מתפלל לפניך : להיות עיניך פתוחית אל הבית הזה יומם ולילה "Have respect to the prayer of Thy servant and to his supplication, O Lord, my God, and hearken unto the cry and the prayer which Thy servant prayeth before Thee; that Thine eyes may be upon this *house* day and night." (2 Ch., vi.)

May a spirit of the most sincere and fervent devotion animate our minds the moment we enter within the sacred portals of this edifice which we are this day consecrating. May the world and all its blighting influences be left outside the porch. May we come with hearts full of thankfulness that Thou hast prepared this temple for us, and permitted us to assemble in it for Thy worship. May we ever be filled with a due sense of our own inferiority and of Thy supreme Majesty, in whose presence the very pillars of heaven tremble. May we clothe our hearts with the garment of reverence, and may we reflect that we are about to perform a duty which cannot be discharged with becoming fitness even by the angels above. Let us bend down our hearts before the Eternal, and say ושמעת אל רחנוני עבדך ועמך ישראל אשר יתפללו אל המקום הזה ואתה תשמע ממקום שבתך מן השמים ושמעת וסלחת : (שם פסוק כ'). "Hearken unto the supplication of Thy servant and of Thy people Israel which they shall make from this place. Hear Thou from Thy dwelling-place, even from heaven, and when Thou hearest forgive."

Yes, O righteous and merciful Judge, hearken to us when we beseech Thee on those ימים נוראים most solemn and awful days which are approaching us, and forgive each one of us the offences he has committed against Thee. We know that our transgressions have been numerous, and that we have merited many, aye very many, punishments by reason of our ingratitude. We make humble acknowledgment to Thee this day for all our sins. ארחה לבדך ידערת את לבב בני האדם "Thou alone knowest the hearts of the children of men." Thou, therefore, O Eternal, canst see our sincerity. Bless, therefore, Thy people, from the highest to the lowest. And bless those whom Thou hast placed in authority over us. Bless us, Thy children, who have built this temple for Thee, and are now devoting it to Thy service. If in other ways we have slighted Thee, let this temple make some reparation for our neglect. Let our hearts be enlarged even as we have enlarged our temple, and let us feel a delight in contributing liberally to its maintenance and support. Let us and our children learn from the words of wisdom that we shall hear in this place to love Thee for Thy goodness, and to fear Thee for Thy majesty. Speak Thou with Thy silent yet potent voice unto our hearts—speak unto Thy people. למען יראוך ללכת בדרכיך כל הימים אשר הם חיים על פני הא־מה "That they may fear Thee, to walk in Thy ways, so long as they live in the land."

Teach us all to love one another for the sake of Thee, and to be kind to one another for the love of Thee, so that when the hour shall come for the temple of our mortal body to be destroyed, having so frequently before exclaimed ה' אהברתי וכו' we may have our thoughts fixed on another temple המכון למעלה which is above —a temple before which the gorgeous splendors of the noblest of temples would sink into utter nothingness—the glorious temple of heaven, which is for ever filled with the presence of the Eternal, and in which the souls of the just shall live for ever. Grant, O Father Eternal, that all of us who are here assembled, and all belonging to us may inherit this mercy, and share in this crowning blessing of all blessings. Amen.

ADVERTISEMENT.

THE Executive Officers of the EAST MELBOURNE HEBREW CONGREGATION acknowledge with thanks Original Donations promised to the Building Fund, as also Amounts Offered at the Consecration of the New Synagogue, Albert-street, on Wednesday, the 5th September, 1877 :—

	Former Donations.			At Consecration.			Total.		
	£	s.	d.	£	s.	d.	£	s.	d.
Mr. Henri J. Hart	73	10	0	31	10	0	105	0	0
„ A. Waxman	52	10	0	21	0	0	73	10	0
„ M. Herman	52	10	0	...			52	10	0
The late Edward Cohen ...	52	10	0	...			52	10	0
Mr. S. De Beer	31	10	0	5	5	0	36	15	0
„ Mark Marks	25	0	0	5	5	0	30	5	0
„ H. Marks	25	0	0	3	3	0	28	3	0
„ Jos. Cohen	26	10	0	1	1	0	27	11	0
„ M. Michaelis	20	0	0	5	5	0	25	5	0
„ L. Levin	25	0	0	...			25	0	0
„ Woolf Davis	...			25	0	0	25	0	0
„ J. Kronheimer	21	0	0	3	3	0	24	3	0
„ E. Rich	...			21	0	0	21	0	0
„ A. Goldberg, Drummond-street	15	15	0	5	5	0	21	0	0
Mr. L. Kraetzer	10	10	0	10	10	0	21	0	0
„ P. Perlstein and family ...	10	10	0	10	10	0	21	0	0
Messrs. Crouch and Wilson ..	15	0	0	10	0	0	25	0	0
The late M. Peter	17	2	0	...			17	2	0
Mr. L. C. Gerschel	15	15	0	...			15	15	0
„ E. Steinfeld	10	10	0	5	5	0	15	15	0
„ B. Barnett	10	10	0	2	2	0	12	12	0
Messrs. M. Tartakover and Son	10	0	0	2	2	0	12	2	0
Mr. M. Harris...	10	10	0	1	1	0	11	11	0
„ A. Stern	10	10	0	...			10	10	0
„ L. Allen	10	10	0	...			10	10	0
Mrs. L. Allen	10	10	0	...			10	10	0
Mr. S. Aaron	10	10	0	...			10	10	0
„ R. Barnard	5	5	0	5	5	0	10	10	0
„ I. Benjamin	10	10	0	...			10	10	0
Dr. J. G. Beaney	10	10	0	...			10	10	0
Mr. Moton Moss	10	10	0	...			10	10	0
Messrs. Warwick Bros. ...	10	10	0	...			10	10	0
Messrs. Delbridge and Thomas	...			10	10	0	10	10	0
Mr. H. Block	...			10	0	0	10	0	0
„ Lionel Marks	...			10	0	0	10	0	0
„ J. Hallerstein	5	5	0	3	3	0	8	8	0
„ A. Barnard	5	5	0	2	2	0	7	7	0

ADVERTISEMENT.

	Former Donations.			At Consecration.			Total.		
	£	s.	d.	£	s.	d.	£	s.	d.
Mr. S. Jacobson	5	5	0	2	2	0	7	7	0
„ and Mrs. B. Isaacs	5	5	0	2	2	0	7	7	0
Messrs. Myers and Zox	3	3	0	4	4	0	7	7	0
Mr. M. Bentwich	5	5	0	1	1	0	6	6	0
„ M. Cohen	5	5	0	0	10	6	5	15	6
„ J. Jones	5	5	0	1	1	0	6	6	0
„ L. Samuel	5	0	0	1	0	0	6	0	0
„ M. Moses	5	5	0	0	10	6	5	15	6
„ B. Sniders	5	5	0	0	10	6	5	15	6
„ A. K. Trouson	5	5	0	0	10	6	5	15	6
„ M. Aron	5	5	0	...			5	5	0
„ D. Altson	5	5	0	...			5	5	0
„ H. Allen	5	5	0	...			5	5	0
„ D. Barnard	5	5	0	...			5	5	0
Messrs. Bentwich and Co.	5	5	0	...			5	5	0
Dr. Balls-Headley	5	5	0	...			5	5	0
Mr. S. Barnett	5	5	0	...			5	5	0
„ H. Coleman	5	5	0	...			5	5	0
„ J. Daley	5	5	0	...			5	5	0
„ L. Davis	5	5	0	...			5	5	0
„ F. Ehrman	5	5	0	...			5	5	0
„ J. Gerson	5	5	0	...			5	5	0
„ J. F. Gunsler	5	5	0	...			5	5	0
„ H. Glauce	5	5	0	...			5	5	0
„ S. Harris	5	5	0	...			5	5	0
„ A. Harris	5	5	0	...			5	5	0
„ J. Harris	5	5	0	...			5	5	0
„ J. Heymanson	5	5	0	...			5	5	0
„ M. Jacobson	5	5	0	...			5	5	0
„ I. Joel	5	5	0	...			5	5	0
Messrs. A. and L. Lesser	5	5	0	...			5	5	0
Mr. B. Lazarus	5	5	0	...			5	5	0
Messrs. Levi Brothers	5	5	0	...			5	5	0
Mr. G. Meares	5	0	0	...			5	0	0
„ G. Magnus	5	5	0	...			5	5	0
„ N. Levi	5	5	0	...			5	5	0
„ Joseph Levy	5	5	0	...			5	5	0
„ J. Monro	5	5	0	...			5	5	0
„ J. Phillips	5	5	0	...			5	5	0
„ J. Paterson	5	0	0	...			5	0	0
„ S Soleberg	5	5	0	...			5	5	0
„ A. Sternberg	5	5	0	15	15	0	21	0	0
„ S. Sternberg	3	3	0	2	2	0	5	5	0
„ L. Saunders	5	0	0	...			5	0	0

ADVERTISEMENT.

	Former Donations.			At Consecration.			Total.		
	£	s.	d.	£	s.	d.	£	s.	d.
Mr. M. Woolff...	5	5	0	..			5	5	0
Mr. J. Wittowski	5	5	0	...			5	5	0
Mr. A. Benjamin	3	3	0	3	3	0	6	6	0
Messrs. P. Falk and Co.	3	3	0	2	2	0	5	5	0
Messrs. Paterson, Laing and Co.	5	5	0	...			5	5	0
Mr. Carl Franklin	...			5	5	0	5	5	0
Messrs. Dodgshun and Co.	5	5	0	...			5	5	0
Messrs. M'Arthur, M'Millan, and Co.	5	5	0	...			5	5	0
Messrs. L. Stevenson and Sons	5	5	0	...			5	5	0
Messrs. Banks Brothers, Bell, and Co.	5	5	0	...			5	5	0
Messrs. Wiseman Bros.	5	5	0	...			5	5	0
Mr. Moses Benjamin	...			5	5	0	5	5	0
Messrs. Loel and Cantor	5	5	0	...			5	5	0
Mr. Isaac Jacobs	...			5	5	0	5	5	0
Messrs. P. Hayman and Sons	...			5	5	0	5	5	0
Mr. S. Benjamin, London	...			5	5	0	5	5	0
„ S. Finklestein	...			5	0	0	5	0	0
„ B. Benjamin	2	2	0	2	2	0	4	4	0
„ I. Michael	3	3	0	1	1	0	4	4	0
„ J. Lyons	2	2	0	2	2	0	4	4	0
„ E. Samuel	4	4	0	...			4	4	0
„ S. Greenberg	3	3	0	1	1	0	4	4	0
„ M. J. Sloman	1	1	0	3	3	0	4	4	0
„ W. Visbord	3	3	0	1	1	0	4	4	0
„ B. Marks	3	3	0	0	10	6	3	13	0
„ D. Walker	3	3	0	0	10	6	3	13	0
„ Max Kronheimer	...			3	3	0	3	3	0
Messrs. Connell, Hogarth, and Co.	3	3	0	...			3	3	0
Mr. B. Josephson	3	3	0	...			3	3	0
„ E. P. Levy	3	3	0	...			3	3	0
„ J. Matheson	3	3	0	...			3	3	0
Dr. Wilkie	3	3	0	...			3	3	0
Messrs. Whitney, Chambers and Co.	3	3	0	...			3	3	0
Mr. J. Davis	3	3	0	...			3	3	0
Messrs. Rosenthal, Aaaronson, and Co.	...			3	3	0	3	3	0
Mr. and Mrs. Mark Moss	...			3	3	0	3	3	0
Mr. and Mrs. J. Solomon	...			3	0	0	3	0	0

	Former Donations.			At Consecration.			Total.		
	£	s.	d.	£	s.	d.	£	s.	d.
Mr. M. Simon	2	2	0	0	10	6	2	12	6
„ J. S. Buchner	2	2	0	0	10	6	2	12	6
„ J. Davis	2	2	0	0	10	6	2	12	6
„ M. Davis	2	2	0	0	10	6	2	12	6
„ A. Fryberg	2	2	0	0	10	6	2	12	6
„ S. Goldschmidt	2	2	0	0	10	6	2	12	6
„ M. Levy	2	2	0	0	10	6	2	12	6
„ M. Nettleberg	2	2	0	0	10	6	2	12	6
„ Myer Rintel	2	2	0	0	10	6	2	12	6
„ Charles Levy	2	2	0	0	10	6	2	12	6
„ J. Levy	2	0	0	1	1	0	3	1	0
„ J. Barnett	2	2	0	0	5	0	2	7	0
„ A. Pinkus	2	2	0	0	5	0	2	7	0
„ B. Allen	2	2	0	...			2	2	0
„ P. Blashki	2	2	0	...			2	2	0
„ A. Brodie	2	2	0	...			2	2	0
„ H. Cohen	2	2	0	...			2	2	0
„ A. Campi	2	2	0	...			2	2	0
Messrs. Chambers and Clutten	2	2	0	...			2	2	0
Mr. H. Gerson	2	2	0	...			2	2	0
Messrs. Eunson and Andrews	2	2	0	...			2	2	0
Mr. A. Harris	2	2	0	...			2	2	0
„ W. Highett	2	2	0	...			2	2	0
„ S. Hamburgher	2	2	0	...			2	2	0
„ J. Hollander	1	1	0	1	1	0	2	2	0
„ J. Hood	2	2	0	...			2	2	0
„ A. M. Jacobs	2	2	0	...			2	2	0
„ M. Krakowski	2	2	0	...			2	2	0
„ H. Levinson	2	2	0	...			2	2	0
Messrs. H. and B. Levy	2	2	0	...			2	2	0
Mr. J. F. Levien	2	2	0	...			2	2	0
„ C. Marks	2	2	0	...			2	2	0
„ A. Levi	1	1	0	1	1	0	2	2	0
„ H. Miller	2	2	0	...			2	2	0
„ M. Monash	2	2	0	...			2	2	0
„ D. E. M'Dougall	2	2	0	...			2	2	0
„ P. G. Pendegrast	2	2	0	...			2	2	0
„ P. Philipson	2	2	0	...			2	2	0
„ P. S. Phillips	2	2	0	...			2	2	0
„ W. Peterson	2	2	0	...			2	2	0
„ S. Rosenbloom	2	2	0	...			2	2	0
„ Robertson	1	1	0	1	1	0	2	2	0
„ Max Roth	2	2	0	...			2	2	0

ADVERTISEMENT.

	Former Donations			At Consecration.			Total.		
	£	s.	d.	£	s.	d.	£	s.	d.
Messrs. Tronson and Rutherford	2	2	0	...			2	2	0
Mr. J. Thompson	2	2	0	...			2	2	0
,, A. A. Samuel	2	2	0	...			2	2	0
,, M. Unger	1	1	0	1	1	0	2	2	0
,, H. Rosenbloom	2	2	0	...			2	2	0
,, A. Smith	2	2	0	...			2	2	0
Messrs. Felton, Grimwade	2	2	0	...			2	2	0
,, Fenwick Bros.	2	2	0	...			2	2	0
,, W. Watson and Sons	2	2	0	...			2	2	0
,, Weaver, Craig, and Orrock	1	1	0	1	1	0	2	2	0
Mrs. E. Rich	...			2	2	0	2	2	0
Mrs. H. Schlam	2	0	0	...			2	0	0
Messrs. W. M'Culloch and Co.	2	2	0	...			2	2	0
Mr. A. K. Smith	...			2	2	0	2	2	0
,, Gavan Gibson	...			2	2	0	2	2	0
Mrs. J. Davis	...			2	2	0	2	2	0
Mrs. H. Marks	...			2	2	0	2	2	0
Mr. A. Pollack	...			2	2	0	2	2	0
,, Mr. E. Brett	...			2	0	0	2	0	0
,, R. J. Harvey	...			2	0	0	2	0	0
,, L. Zucker	...			2	2	0	2	2	0
,, S. Moss	...			2	2	0	2	2	0
,, M Capua	...			2	2	0	2	2	0
,, A. Levy	...			2	2	0	2	2	0
,, M. Simmons	...			2	0	0	2	0	0
,, D. Abrahams	...			2	2	0	2	2	0
,, J. Barnard	...			2	2	0	2	2	0
,, Alfred Levy	...			2	2	0	2	2	0
Mrs. Finklestein	...			2	0	0	2	0	0
Mr. and Mrs. C. Harris	...			2	2	0	2	2	0
Messrs. Cohn Brothers	...			2	2	0	2	2	0
Mr. C. Primer	...			2	2	0	2	2	0
,, J. Caro	...			2	2	0	2	2	0
,, A. Brasch	2	0	0	...			2	0	0
,, T. S. Bellair	2	0	0	...			2	0	0
,, S. Jacobs	1	1	0	0	10	6	1	11	6
,, A. M. Isaacs	1	1	0	0	10	6	1	11	6
,, L. Moss	1	1	0	0	10	6	1	11	6
,, M. Moses and daughters	1	11	6	...			1	11	6
,, J. Sagel	1	1	0	0	10	6	1	11	6
,, R. Bodington	1	1	0	0	10	6	1	11	6

ADVERTISEMENT.

	Former Donations.			At Consecration.			Total.		
	£	s.	d.	£	s.	d.	£	s.	d.
Mrs. and Miss Bloch		...		1	10	0	1	10	0
Mr. M. Stalkowski	1	1	0	0	5	0	1	6	0
Mrs. B. Marks	1	1	0	0	5	0	1	6	0
Mr. K. Abrahams	1	1	0		...		1	1	0
„ M. Abrahams	1	1	0		...		1	1	0
„ L. A. Abrahams	1	1	0		...		1	1	0
„ P. H. Benjamin	1	1	0		...		1	1	0
„ A. Benjamin	1	1	0		...		1	1	0
„ H. Benjamin	1	1	0		...		1	1	0
„ A. E. Benjamin	1	1	0		...		1	1	0
Miss Benjamin	1	1	0		...		1	1	0
Mrs. P. Blashki	1	1	0		...		1	1	0
Mr. L. Berwick	1	1	0		...		1	1	0
„ L. Aarons	1	1	0		...		1	1	0
Messrs. Buckley and Nunn	1	1	0		...		1	1	0
Mr. J. Bernstein	1	1	0		...		1	1	0
„ F. Cohen	1	1	0		...		1	1	0
Mrs. Ed. Cohen		...		1	1	0	1	1	0
Mr. M. Crawcour	1	1	0		...		1	1	0
„ Mr. Dynon	1	1	0		...		1	1	0
„ A. Ellis	1	1	0		...		1	1	0
„ S. Flock	1	1	0		...		1	1	0
„ S. Franklin	1	1	0		...		1	1	0
Mrs. Falk	1	1	0		...		1	1	0
Dr. Figg	1	1	0		...		1	1	0
Mr. E. G. Fitzgibbon	1	1	0		...		1	1	0
G. H.	1	1	0		...		1	1	0
Mr. P. Hyams	1	1	0		...		1	1	0
„ H. Heymanson	1	1	0		...		1	1	0
Messrs. Halstead and Kerr	1	1	0		...		1	1	0
Mr. R. Hodgson	1	1	0		...		1	1	0
Master Joel	1	1	0		...		1	1	0
Mr. A. Kasner	1	1	0		...		1	1	0
„ M. Kovolski	0	10	6	0	10	6	1	1	0
„ S. Kozminski	1	1	0		...		1	1	0
„ L. Levy	1	1	0		...		1	1	0
„ H. Loel	1	1	0		...		1	1	0
„ B. Marks	1	1	0		...		1	1	0
„ S. Moses	1	1	0		...		1	1	0
„ M. Moses, jun.	1	1	0		...		1	1	0
„ J. Marks	1	1	0		...		1	1	0
„ D. Lyons	1	1	0		...		1	1	0
„ L. Levy	1	1	0		...		1	1	0

ADVERTISEMENT.

	Former Donations.			At Consecration.			Total.		
	£	s.	d.	£	s.	d.	£	s.	d.
Mr. D. Lobascher	1	1	0	...			1	1	0
,, J. Magner	1	1	0	...			1	1	0
,, J. M'Ewan	1	1	0	...			1	1	0
,, S. Nathan	1	1	0	...			1	1	0
Master J. Phillips	1	1	0	...			1	1	0
Dr. Rowan	1	1	0	...			1	1	0
Mr. S. Solomon	1	1	0	...			1	1	0
,, M. Saunders	1	1	0	...			1	1	0
,, S. Traxberg	1	1	0	...			1	1	0
,, G. Samson	1	1	0	...			1	1	0
,, B. Solomon	1	1	0	...			1	1	0
,, M. Brodzky	...			1	1	0	1	1	0
,, J. Cohen	...			1	1	0	1	1	0
,, A. Levy	...			1	1	0	1	1	0
Messrs. Stevenson and Elliott	1	1	0	...			1	1	0
Mr. P. Windmiller	1	1	0	...			1	1	0
,, J. Joseph	1	1	0	...			1	1	0
,, Hurry	1	1	0	...			1	1	0
,, J. Wertheim	1	1	0	...			1	1	0
,, J. Joseph	1	1	0	...			1	1	0
Messrs. T. Martin and Co.	1	1	0	...			1	1	0
Mr. J. Fletcher	1	1	0	...			1	1	0
Messrs. W. Henderson and Co.	1	1	0	...			1	1	0
Messrs. Warne and Reid	1	1	0	...			1	1	0
,, M'Coey and Co.	1	1	0	...			1	1	0
,, Cochrane and O'Brien	1	1	0	...			1	1	0
Mr. A. Kasner	1	1	0	...			1	1	0
Mrs. S. Phillips	1	1	0	...			1	1	0
Mr. P. Bloom	1	1	0	...			1	1	0
Mrs. L. Zucker	...			1	1	0	1	1	0
Major Smith	...			1	1	0	1	1	0
The Misses Rich	...			1	1	0	1	1	0
Mrs. A. Loel	...			1	1	0	1	1	0
,, A. Barnard	...			1	1	0	1	1	0
,, F. Ehrman	...			1	1	0	1	1	0
,, S. Moss	...			1	1	0	1	1	0
Mr. J. Grimwald	...			1	1	0	1	1	0
Miss Barnett	...			1	1	0	1	1	0
Mrs. Moton Moss	...			1	1	0	1	1	0
Mr. Herman Levy	...			1	1	0	1	1	0
,, Joseph Benjamin	...			1	1	0	1	1	0
Messrs. Kaufman Bros.	...			1	1	0	1	1	0

ADVERTISEMENT.

	Former Donations.			At Consecration.			Total.		
	£	s.	d.	£	s.	d.	£	s.	d.
Mr. M. Rosenfeld				1	1	0	1	1	0
Mrs. John Moses				1	1	0	1	1	0
Mr. A. Loel				11	11	0	11	11	0
„ J. Lazarus				1	1	0	1	1	0
„ D. P. Piser				1	1	0	1	1	0
„ A. Solomon				1	1	0	1	1	0
Mrs. Joseph Cohen				1	1	0	1	1	0
„ E. H. Simeon				1	1	0	1	1	0
„ S. Leon				6	6	0	6	6	0
Mr. W. Flegeltaub				1	1	0	1	1	0
„ J. Sternberg				1	1	0	1	1	0
„ Ed. Marks				1	1	0	1	1	0
„ J. Levy				1	1	0	1	1	0
„ L. Saunders				1	1	0	1	1	0
„ L. Levinson				1	1	0	1	1	0
Messrs. Davy and Cole				1	1	0	1	1	0
Mr. L. H. Phillips				1	1	0	1	1	0
„ J. Lipshut				1	1	0	1	1	0
„ B. Levy				1	1	0	1	1	0
„ A. Goldberg				1	1	0	1	1	0
„ J. Bloomberg				1	1	0	1	1	0
„ H. Marks				1	1	0	1	1	0
„ J. Marks				1	1	0	1	1	0
Mrs. W. Davis				1	1	0	1	1	0
Mr. L. H. Hart				1	1	0	1	1	0
„ A. Levy				1	1	0	1	1	0
„ and Mrs. Bernard Marks				1	1	0	1	1	0
„ J. Walde				1	1	0	1	1	0
„ I. Barnet				1	1	0	1	1	0
„ E. Duckett				1	1	0	1	1	0
„ M. Jacobs				1	1	0	1	1	0
„ D. Hecksher				1	0	0	1	0	0
Mrs. R. Barnard				1	0	0	1	0	0
Mr. G. Alexander	1	0	0				1	0	0
„ A. Cohen	1	0	0				1	0	0
„ B. Nathan	1	0	0				1	0	0
„ L. Solomon	1	0	0				1	0	0
Mrs. and Miss Goodheim				1	0	0	1	0	0
Mr. A. Hosking				1	0	0	1	0	0
„ J. H. Anderson				1	0	0	1	0	0
„ J. Purvis				1	0	0	1	0	0
Miss Amelia Finklestein				1	0	0	1	0	0
„ Eva Finklestein				1	0	0	1	0	0

ADVERTISEMENT.

	Former Donations.			At Consecration.			Total.		
	£	s.	d.	£	s.	d.	£	s.	d.
Master H. Finklestein	...	...		1	0	0	1	0	0
Dr. L. L. Smith	...	...		1	0	0	1	0	0
Messrs. J. M'Gee and Co.	...	..		1	0	0	1	0	0
Mrs. A. Goldberg	...	...		0	10	6	0	10	6
Mr. N. J. Dias	0	10	6	...			0	10	6
,, E. Doyle	0	10	6	...			0	10	6
,, S. Davis	0	10	6	...			0	10	6
,, M. Levinson	0	10	6	...			0	10	6
,, W. Lazarus	0	10	6	..			0	10	6
,, J. Levy	0	10	6	...			0	10	6
,, I. Levy	0	10	6	...			0	10	6
,, M. Marks	0	10	6	...			0	10	6
,, T. Martin	0	10	6	...			0	10	6
,, Stewart O'Brien	0	10	6	...			0	10	6
,, R. Robertson	0	10	6	..			0	10	6
,, S. Samuels	0	10	6	...			0	10	6
,, A. M. Simmons	0	10	6	...			0	10	6
,, J. F. Whittey	0	10	0	...			0	10	0
,, E. Rintel	0	10	6	...			0	10	6
Mrs. L. Lazarus	0	10	0	...			0	10	0
Miss Lazarus	0	10	0	...			0	10	0
A Friend	0	10	0	...			0	10	0
Mr. P. Levy	...			0	10	6	0	10	6
Mrs. S. Tartakover	...			0	10	6	0	10	6
Mr. H. Venable	...			0	10	0	0	10	0
,, H. J. Alexander	...			0	10	6	0	10	6
,, M. A. Papkin	...			0	10	6	0	10	6
,, M. L. Woolff	...			0	10	6	0	10	6
,, D. Miranda	...			0	10	6	0	10	6
,, B. Harris	...			0	10	6	0	10	6
,, H. Neustadt	...			0	10	6	0	10	6
Mrs. J. Michael	...			0	10	6	0	10	6
,, Mosely Hyman	...			0	10	6	0	10	6
,, D. Abrahams	...			0	10	6	0	10	6
,, M. Jacobson	...			0	10	6	0	10	6
,, A. Sherman	...			0	10	6	0	10	6
Mr. J. Matthews	...			0	10	6	0	10	6
,, S. Williams	...			0	10	6	0	10	6
Miss Barnard	...			0	10	0	0	10	0
Mrs. M. Marks	...			0	10	6	0	10	6
Miss S. Moss	...			0	10	6	0	10	6
Mrs. D. E. Piser	...			0	10	0	0	10	0
Mr. B. Emanuel	...			0	10	6	0	10	6

ADVERTISEMENT.

	Former Donations.			At Consecration			Total.		
	£	s.	d.	£	s.	d.	£	s.	d.
Mrs. M. Moses		...		0	10	6	0	10	6
Miss Davis		...		0	10	0	0	10	0
Mr. L. Waterman		...		0	10	0	0	10	0
„ J. Simmons		...		0	10	0	0	10	0
Mrs. S. Soleberg		...		0	10	6	0	10	6
„ H. Marks		...		0	10	6	0	10	6
„ Kuthe		...		0	10	6	0	10	6
Mr. Maurice Marks		...		0	10	6	0	10	6
„ S. B. Saunders		...		0	10	6	0	10	6
Master B. Marks		...		0	10	6	0	10	6
Mr. H. Wolfman		...		0	10	6	0	10	6
„ S. Solomon		...		0	10	6	0	10	6
Mrs. M. Tartakover		...		0	10	6	0	10	6
Mr. L. H. Hart		...		0	10	6	0	10	6
„ A. Levy		...		0	10	6	0	10	6
„ J. Avinsky		...		0	10	6	0	10	6
Mrs. Nettleberg		...		0	10	6	0	10	6
Mr. and Mrs. M. Levy		...		0	10	6	0	10	6
„ S. Isaacs		...		0	10	6	0	10	6
Mrs. A. L. Levy		...		0	10	6	0	10	6
Mr. H. Cohen		...		0	10	6	0	10	6
Miss Cronson	0	5	0		...		0	5	0
Mr. J. Ellis	0	5	0		...		0	5	0
A Friend	0	5	0		...		0	5	0
Mr. E. Harris	0	5	0		...		0	5	0
Mrs. Moses	0	5	0		...		0	5	0
Mr. J. Marks	0	5	0		...		0	5	0
Miss Marks	0	5	0		...		0	5	0
Mr. L. Pollack	0	5	0		...		0	5	0
„ A. Simmons	0	5	0		...		0	5	0
Miss S. Phillips		...		0	5	0	0	5	0
„ Jude		...		0	5	0	0	5	0
„ C. Marks		...		0	5	0	0	5	0
Mr. D. Sonnenberg		...		0	5	0	0	5	0
„ S. L. Fryberg		...		0	5	0	0	5	0
Mrs. Harris		...		0	5	0	0	5	0
Miss A. Phillips		...		0	5	0	0	5	0
Mrs. S. Belinfante		...		0	5	0	0	5	0
„ S. Goldschmidt		...		0	5	0	0	5	0
Mr. L. Davis		...		0	5	0	0	5	0
Miss C. Moses		...		0	5	0	0	5	0
„ M. Davis		...		0	5	0	0	5	0
Mr. J. Rutherford		...		0	5	0	0	5	0

ADVERTISEMENT.

	Former Donations			At Consecration.			Total.		
	£	s.	d.	£	s.	d.	£	s.	d.
Mr. E. Harvey	...			0	5	0	0	5	0
Miss C. Davis	...			0	5	0	0	5	0
Mrs. P. Phillips	...			0	5	0	0	5	0
Mr. E. Fruhauf	...			0	5	0	0	5	0
Sundry amounts	...			1	2	6	1	2	6
Cash collections	...			18	0	0	18	0	0
Additional subscriptions—									
Mr J. Solomon	...			...			2	2	0
,, and Mrs. H. Lyons	...			...			1	1	0
,, J. Holton	...			...			1	1	0
,, J. O'Brady	...			...			0	10	0
,, E. F. Tronson	...			...			0	5	0
,, J. M'Lellan	...			...			0	5	0
,, M. J. Cohen	...			...			1	1	0
,, D. S. Phillips	...			...			0	10	6
,, A. Anderson	...			...			1	0	0
Messrs. Wisewould and Gibbs	...			...			5	5	0
Mr. J. Adamson	...			...			1	0	0
,, C. Anderson	...			...			1	1	0
,, J. Band	...			...			0	10	6
,, J. Fergusson	...			...			0	10	0
,, W. Alexander	...			...			2	2	0
,, J. A. Smith	...			...			1	1	0
Messrs. Fenwick Bros.	...			...			2	2	0
Mr. M. Jacobs	...			...			1	1	0
,, T. M'Dermott	...			...			1	1	0
,, A. Levy	...			...			1	1	0

M. HYMAN, Secretary.

www.ingramcontent.com/pod-product-compliance
Lightning Source LLC
Chambersburg PA
CBHW020245090426
42735CB00010B/1845